⚐ W9-COY-789

GOLDRUSH PRODUCTS COMPANY
491 WEST SAN CARLOS STREET
SAN JOSE, CA 95110-2632
408/288-4090 ♦ FAX: 408/286-1503

| Great in |
| Bread Makers |

RETAIL PRICE LIST

GOLDRUSH SOURDOUGH PRODUCTS

DATE
JAN 93

ITEM	DESCRIPTION	NET WT. OZ		

INSTANT MIXES (CANISTERS) - GOLDRUSH
NO CHOLESTEROL - REDUCED FAT - JUST ADD WATER

ITEM	DESCRIPTION	NET WT. OZ	Price	
2321	SOURDOUGH PANCAKE/WAFFLE	24	$ 5.00	1 Case/9 Canisters
2323	SOURDOUGH FRENCH BREAD	24	$ 5.00	$22.50+$9.98 Frt.
2325	SOURDOUGH BRAN MUFFINS	24	$ 5.00	No Handling Charge
2326	SOURDOUGH BISCUIT	24	$ 5.00	

INSTANT MIXES (BOXES) - GOLDRUSH
NO CHOLESTEROL - REDUCED FAT - JUST ADD WATER

ITEM	DESCRIPTION	NET WT. OZ	Price	
2201	SOURDOUGH PANCAKE/WAFFLE	20	$ 4.00	
2203	SOURDOUGH FRENCH BREAD	20	$ 3.50	
2205	SOURDOUGH BRAN MUFFIN	20	$ 4.00	
2206	SOURDOUGH BISCUIT	20	$ 3.50	1 Case/12 Pkg
2207	SOURDOUGH CORNBREAD & MUFFIN	20	$ 3.50	$24.00+$11.50 Frt.
2208	SOURDOUGH OATMEAL MUFFIN & COOKIE	20	$ 4.00	No Handling Charge
2209	SOURDOUGH MULTIGRAIN	20	$ 4.00	
210	SOURDOUGH BELGIAN WAFFLE	20	$ 4.00	
2212	SOURDOUGH LEMON POUND CAKE	20	$ 4.00	

NEW ♦♦**INSTANT MIXES (BAGS)**♦♦ GOLDRUSH COUNTRY CLASSIC ♦ JUST ADD WATER OR BEER

GREAT IN 1, 1 1/2, or 2 POUND BREAD MACHINES OR BY CONVENTIONAL METHODS!

ITEM	DESCRIPTION	NET WT. OZ	Price	
2214	SOURDOUGH BEER BREAD	18	$ 3.90	
2215	SOURDOUGH GARLIC BEER BREAD	18	$ 3.90	12 Pkg - Single Variety
2216	SOURDOUGH '9' GRAIN BEER BREAD	18	$ 3.90	$23.40 + $10.00 Frt.
2217	SOURDOUGH WHOLE WHEAT BEER BREAD	18	$ 3.90	No Handling Charge
2218	SOURDOUGH ONION-DILL BEER BREAD	18	$ 3.90	
0219	SOURDOUGH RYE BEER BREAD	18	$ 3.90	
2222	SAMPLER CASE CONTAINS:	18	$26.00+ $10.00 Frt.	
	(2) 2214, 2215, 2218, 2219, 2220, 2216, 2217		No Handling Charge	

SOURDOUGH STARTER & ACCESSORIES - GOLDRUSH

ITEM	DESCRIPTION	NET WT. OZ	Price	
1001	SOURDOUGH STARTER PACKET	.5	$ 3.15	
1001A	ALASKA SOURDOUGH STARTER PACKET	.5	$ 3.15	
1004	COOKBOOK WITH STARTER GIFT PACK	..	$12.00	
1005	SOURDOUGH COOKBOOK	..	$10.00	
1006	BEGINNERS BOX (20 oz CROCK & STARTER)	20	$16.00	
1007	ADVENTURE BOX (20 oz CROCK, BOOK & STARTER)	20	$22.00	
1008	JUNIOR CROCK (12 oz CROCK & STARTER)	12	$10.00	

NEW! BAKER'S HELPER VITAL WHEAT GLUTEN BREAD RECIPES "RISE" MORE, BREADING & BATTER STICK, PIZZA DOUGH STRETCHES MORE

ITEM	DESCRIPTION	NET WT. OZ	Price	
2901	VITAL WHEAT GLUTEN	16	$5.00	

TO ORDER

Available at your favorite store or ask them to order it.
Send order with a check made payable to Goldrush at the above address.
Include payment for the items ordered, freight (15% of the order total). Include $2.00 for handling.

Please allow 2-6 weeks for delivery.

Adventures in
SOURDOUGH COOKING
&
BAKING

By Charles D. Wilford

Published by:

GOLDRUSH PRODUCTS COMPANY

491 West San Carlos St. San Jose, California 95110-2632

Acknowledgement

Cover: Jerry Otwell - Rutledge

This book incorporates material formerly published under the title of "Adventures in San Francisco Sourdough Cooking & Baking"

ISBN 0 — 912936 — 00 — 2

Dedication

This book is dedicated to Helen Blair Boyd. Without her the book would not have been possible. Her years of baking experience have been invaluable in providing clear, easy to follow recipes. Her own recipes have immeasurably enriched this cookbook. Her untiring energy and skills in the testing kitchen have insured the high quality and reliability of each recipe. For all these reasons and many more this book is dedicated to her.

Table of Contents

Chapter 1
Your Sourdough Adventure

Congratulations! You are about to start your sourdough adventure. You will find that sourdough cooking and baking is great fun and that you can create delicious baked goods for your family, your friends and yourself. This is because your sourdough starter is alive, thus preparation and baking is a greater challenge with correspondingly greater rewards than when using a commercial yeast. However, because it is alive you must treat it carefully and with the great kindness that any living thing deserves. For this reason you will receive maximum benefits in sourdough baking if you read this and the following three chapters before embarking on your sourdough adventure in the kitchen.

Sourdough is nature's leavening agent. It causes pancakes, breads, rolls, muffins, cakes and innumerable other products to rise before and during baking. This rising or leavening action caused by your sourdough starter produces the fine properties found in your baked goods.

Literally thousands of words have been written and published concerning sourdough, its origin and its uses in cooking and baking. Sourdough and its unique leavening properties have been discussed and praised in many publications by many authors. It has been attributed to all manner of beginnings from the fabled Alaskan "sour-dough" to the more humble and less glamorous starter in the sour-dough crock on the back of grandma's cookstove.

We have found mentions of sourdough leavening methods in books describing cooking and baking from the times of the Egyptians. This gives sourdough a birthday about 5,000 years ago. Most Western and neareastern civilizations have used sourdough or a variation of its basic workings for hundreds of years. While the lore behind sourdough is not of concern to us in our adventure, we are interested in the knowledge and techniques developed over the centuries concerning sourdough. Much has already been written about the history of sourdough but not enough concerning the everyday use of sourdough and the recipes that comprise sourdough cooking and baking.

This book is written to furnish you with a complete and useful guide in sourdough cooking and baking. An additional purpose is to provide a description of how sourdough works and lives and the methods necessary to insure its continued good characteristics and longevity. This will guarantee that your sourdough starter will provide you with a lifetime of enjoyment. Thus following this guide will fill your dining table with delicious foods prepared during your sourdough adventure. It will bring back memories of the goodness of old fashioned baking as well it should, since starters were the standard form of leavening in baking in this country up until the advent of commercial yeasts.

The methods, descriptions and recipes in this book are designed both for gourmet cooks with unlimited resources available and perfect cooking and baking conditions at their right hand and also for the average homemaker who must cook under somewhat less than ideal conditions. Few people are blessed with perfect baking conditions. Therefore the recipes on the following pages have been written with an absence of flowery frills and in a manner as down to earth and easy to follow as is possible. The amount of cross referencing required has been held to a minimum. Once you have read the first four chapters in the book you should have fine results from any recipe in the book. They have been written such that no chemicals or commercial yeasts are necessary. In addition you will find hints on how to take your sourdough starter camping with you and how to use it to give you satisfying and filling pancakes, biscuits and breads while in the wilderness.

As you enter your adventure there is one ingredient not listed in any recipe which is absolutely necessary to the success of sourdough cooking and baking. This is large amounts of patience. Unlike modern premixed and additive preserved products, sourdough reverts to the very basics of cooking and baking and one must be patient with the nature of sourdough to achieve good and uniform results. When the recipe specifies that a bread be allowed to rise for two hours many people want to rush things a little, and cheat on the waiting period. Of course, should this be done, the results may not be the same as if one had waited the full time. Are you going to be satisfied with uncertain results? So everyone must practice the somewhat lost art of patience if they are to become really proud of their sourdough products. We can only say that the sheer thrill of accomplishment and the hearty words of praise greeting the serving of your sourdough foods will more than repay you for your patience in preparing them.

Each and every recipe contained in this book has been tested by the authors time and time again under both the best possible kitchen conditions and also in drafty kitchens and using ovens with little temperature control. Each recipe has been tested in both San Francisco and a rural midwest kitchen in order that the recipes will be as well suited for the everyday cook as they are to the gourmet. Each recipe has passed our tests to prove it worthy of inclusion in this book and warrants consideration as part of your sourdough adventure. We have attempted to give you the basic sourdough recipes such as pancakes, waffles and breads plus a well rounded selection of baked goods of other types that are prepared or enhanced with the use of sourdough. In addition to our recipes we encourage your experimentation with other recipes for sourdough cooking and baking and would welcome your comments and ideas to even further sourdough adventures.

As we close this chapter and you prepare to enter Chapter 2 of your adventure in sourdough we want to say that we are confident of your success and satisfaction with the good things that will result from your use of our recipes and that we assure you your journey through the realm of sourdough cooking and baking will be as rewarding to you as it has been for others throughout the world.

Chapter 2
Ingredients, Utensils & Techniques

One of the most important grounds for success in baking is the knowledge of and familiarity with the ingredients included, the characteristics of the pots and pans used in baking and the methods and practices of fine baking. While we cannot hope to be comprehensive we do hope to provide you with a sound background. This knowledge will contribute greatly to baking high quality foods on your sourdough adventure.

This chapter has three sections. These sections cover ingredients, utensils and techniques.

INGREDIENTS

The quality of the ingredients that you use will have a greater effect on your results than any other single factor. For this reason we urge that you always use the best available ingredients for each and every item. Even one mediocre or poor quality item will have a greater effect on the total quality of your finished product than just its share of the ingredients. In other words, the final result will only be as good as the lowest quality ingredient used.

This section, however does not deal with the ingredient that we consider the most important of all. This is of course, the sourdough starter which you will use as a leavener. Sourdough starters will be discussed thoroughly in Chapter 3.

FLOUR

The second most important ingredient in the recipes in this book is flour. It is the major ingredient in bulk in almost every recipe and thus deserves the most detailed discussion.

Wheat flour is the most commonly used flour in this country. It has contributed greatly to the greatness of the United States as a country's strength derives firstly from its ability to feed its many peoples and its armies well. For many years the United States produced the bulk of the wheat flour in the world. It wasn't until the Twentieth Century that hardy types of wheat were developed which would provide abundant harvests in other countries with other climates.

Wheat flour is available in many forms. These different wheat flours are produced from a variety of wheats and by a variety of milling methods. Examination of the whole kernel of wheat and the different milling methods shows us the difference between the various wheat flours. This in turn leads us to an understanding of why the authors specify that the best white wheat flour for our bread recipes is unbleached hard winter white and that the best whole wheat flour is stone ground whole wheat.

The wheat kernel is composed of three major parts. The larger part of the inner portion is called the endosperm. This contains most of the starch and a form of protein which is called gluten. The other inner part is called the embryo or wheat germ. The wheat germ contains high quality protein as well as large amounts of vitamins B and E. It also contains the major portion of the fats. These fats are unsaturated fatty acids which are very important nutritionally. The kernel is covered by several layers of "skin" which are called the bran. The bran also contains large amounts of vitamins and minerals and high quality proteins.

The gluten in the endosperm is a very important item from the point of breadmaking. The gluten is an elastic form of protein. It separates from the starch portion of the endosperm when wet. Its molecules align themselves in long strings when kneaded and form umbrella-like structures. This is the factor which traps the gases produced by the sourdough action and causes the bread to rise and thus achieve a lightness which otherwise would not be possible.

The white flour offered for sale in most supermarkets for bread and cake baking is composed almost entirely of the endosperm portion of the wheat kernel. The bran is removed to increase digestibility and to improve the color while the wheat germ is removed to prevent spoilage.

Without the bran and wheat germ most of the original nutritive qualities of the wheat are not present. Since the remaining part consists mainly of starch we think of breads, especially white breads as extremely fattening. They are fattening only if the natural balance of unsaturated fats, vitamins, minerals and protein has been destroyed or removed during processing. Thus as your sourdough adventures increase you will find that using the right flour will give you a slice of bread that is practically a meal in itself. The natural nutrition of bread made with good flour is the real reason why your home baked bread is really cheaper than a loaf of store bought white bread.

Although the all purpose flour available in your local supermarket may be labeled enriched, usually only four of the many items milled out of the wheat have been restored. In addition it probably has been bleached to provide a uniform color. This is artificial and certainly serves no nutritive purpose. If not performed carefully, bleaching can destroy or partially limit the stretching powers of the gluten. Fresh, unbleached white flour will have a slight yellowish tinge. However, as the flour ages this color will disappear.

All purpose flour is made from a ground blend of hard and soft wheats. The soft wheat contains less gluten than the hard wheat flour. This contains a higher gluten content and has a higher absorptive capacity for water. Together these characteristics mean a lighter more moist bread. However, if used in cakes, you may find an undesired tough elasticity. This can be avoided by sifting the flour 5 or 6 times before adding to the mixture. You may want to use the all purpose flour or possibly even a cake flour (which is made exclusively from a soft wheat) to achieve a more crumbly cake texture.

There are also presifted flours on the market. These flours have been ground very fine and as a result will change the taste and texture of your breads. We do not recommend them as the need for sifting flour when baking bread is questionable due to the fact that the amount of flour needed cannot be exactly measured.

Another type of flour which is now available is the self-rising flour. This is not recommended, as the flour is of no better nutritional quality than the all purpose white flour and in addition it contains chemical leaveners and salt. These chemical leaveners (baking soda and baking powder) are not necessary since sourdough is a leavener. They may cause imbalance of ingredients if used with the recipes in this book.

For all the reasons above we recommend that the white flour called for in the recipes be unbleached hard white wheat flour. This type of flour is now available in many supermarkets. If you cannot find it there, a health food or natural food store is likely to carry it and the other types of flours discussed in the following paragraphs.

Whole wheat flour (called entire wheat flour in some older cookbooks) does not have the bran and the wheat germ removed as does white flour. Since the wheat germ contains fats therefore likely to become rancid quickly, stone ground whole wheat flour should be acquired. During the stone grinding process the fats are spread evenly over the flour thus leaving no fatty concentrations to spoil.

When buying whole wheat flour we recommend stone ground flour for its superior keeping quality and its added nutrition. If you believe that the bran in whole wheat flour is hard to digest then try straining the bran out and soaking it for a few hours in warm water before returning it to the rest of the flour. This should soften the bran enough to make it more easily digested.

Gluten flour is a starch free flour made from high protein wheat flour. Although it changes the taste slightly it can be used at the discretion of the cook in small amounts (¼ cup or less) to provide the additional elasticity necessary to cause bread baked from flours other than those made from wheat to rise to a higher and lighter consistency.

Cracked wheat is cut instead of being ground. The amount of available gluten is not as great as with whole wheat or white flour and thus cannot be used as the only flour in a bread. It should be used with white flour which provides enough gluten to rise properly. In addition it should be soaked in hot water before using to make it more easily digestible.

Wheat germ is sold separately from flour. It can be added to any bread in small amounts replacing other flours up to the amount of 1/4 cup to provide additional food value, flavor and taste. It is also available as a finely ground flour.

Rye flour is the only non-wheat flour which is high in gluten. Rye flour has even more gluten than wheat flour and thus forms a stickier and more elastic dough. Rye frequently makes a suitable replacement for those who are allergic to wheat flour.

Cornmeal is available in both yellow and white forms made from yellow and white corn respectively. Each is available in whole and degermed form. The degermed has the fatty germ removed to enhance its keeping properties. However, this removes much of the food value. Yellow cornmeal has more vitamin A than the white. If you feel that your breads using cornmeal are too grainy try boiling the cornmeal in water or milk before adding it to the other ingredients.

Other flours which can be used are barley, buckwheat, oat, peanut, soy, rice and potato flour.

Flour should be stored in dry areas to prevent moisture from being absorbed. In addition any whole grain flours which contain the germ portion thus contain fats and should always be kept cool. Ideal storage is in sealed plastic bags or containers in the freezer or refrigerator. If space isn't available there, put the flour on a low shelf in the coolest place you can find. Flour should be gently stirred before measuring. This eliminates the need for sifting in the recipes of this book.

YEASTS

Sourdough is a leavening agent. It is composed of billions of tiny microscopic plants. All commercial yeasts are composed of similar types of these tiny organisms. As yeast and sourdough have basically the same form and both serve only as leavening agents we consider commercial yeasts not necessary. It is perishable, expensive and artificially prepared. Sourdough on the other hand is always fresh. It costs a minuscule amount since you save some each time you bake to grow back to its original strength for the next baking. It was originally wild yeast spores which have multiplied and are now controlled as to growth and purity. It contains no preservatives and above all is inexpensive.

CHEMICAL LEAVENERS

Baking soda and baking powder are the principal chemical leaveners in use today. They are used mainly as insurance that the bread will rise and also to cause it to rise more quickly. Baking powder sometimes leaves a bitter taste and will cause a slight yellow tinge to some baked products. As it produces the gases necessary for leavening it leaves behind such compounds as Rochelle Salts, Tataric Acid, alum, lime and ammonia depending on the type used. We do not feel that sourdough needs this help and thus have not included any baking powder in the recipes in this book. Addition of either will not speed up the action of the sourdough nor will it improve the taste of the baked item.

SWEETENERS

Sweeteners aid the proper action of the sourdough in many recipes. They also are an important factor in producing a darker crust. Recipes which call for sugar mean ordinary granulated sugar. However, this may be replaced with raw sugar if you so desire. For a different taste you might try replacing each tablespoon of sugar with one of brown sugar. Or replace each tablespoon of sugar with $\frac{2}{3}$ tablespoon of molasses or honey. Each will give a subtle but very flavorable difference to your bread or pancakes. Sugar aids the action of the sourdough when included in the amounts specified in the recipes. In recipes containing large amounts of sugar be sure to stir well as failure to do so will cause a very dry crumb. If added in larger quantities it will slow this action. Avoid artificial sweeteners as some turn extremely bitter when cooked.

BUTTER & OIL

Most of the recipes in this book which need a fat call for butter. The authors feel that butter is the most desirable of the fats available. Butter may be replaced by an equivalent amount of margarine or vegetable shortening with a slight loss of flavor. For recipes which involve creaming, the replacement of butter by margarine makes the task easier but the result less tasty. Some breads are designed for lard, salad oils, olive oil or soy oil. When they are called for they should be used as the distinctive properties of the oil specified are an integral part of the recipe. However, using any of these oils when butter is called for will cause a distinct change in flavor. Do not use whipped butter in baking as the air whipped into it will give you a false measure.

WATER

Water affects the rising properties of sourdough. Hard water will retard the proper action of the sourdough. The rising times will be extended if hard water is used. On the other hand, very soft water will make your dough very sticky and soggy, thus increasing the difficulty of working with it. If your water has a high hydrogen sulfide (rotten egg) content your sourdough will not work well and you should use bottled water.

UTENSILS

Perhaps the most piece of equipment necessary for sourdough cooking and baking is the thermometer. In fact two thermometers are suggested. A room thermometer is necessary for testing the temperature of your proofing or rising area and an oven thermometer because of the unreliability of most oven thermostats . Most ovens will have a difference of 5 to 50 degrees F. between the actual temperatures and that on the dial which is used to set the temperature. Unless you have a repairman readjust the thermostat every six months it is likely that your oven temperatures are different from those you think they are. Therefore, use a high quality oven thermometer to insure accurate temperatures.

The room thermometer is just as important since your sourdough needs a temperature as close to 85 degrees F. as possible. This temperature causes the sourdough to work at its best. A lower temperature causes it to slow down — while a high temperature is favorable to the growth of the other organisms which might adversely affect the quality of taste of your sourdough products. This temperature is critical to your success.

Since today's kitchens are seldom kept this warm we suggest several methods of achieving the desired temperature. If your oven is gas with a pilot light use a room thermometer to test its temperature with the door open and with the door closed. Choose the position which keeps the temperature as close to 85 degrees F. as possible. Another solution is an oven light which can be left on. Often this will keep your oven at 85 degrees F. A closet in which you can leave a light bulb burning sometimes will keep the desired temperature. A fourth alternative is to put the item to be proofed in an unlit oven with a bowl or pan of hot water below it. This will keep the proper temperature for long periods of time When the temperature begins to drop replace the water with more hot water.

A proofing box is easy to build if you have tools and wood handy. Build a rectangular box with a hinged door big enough to hold a 4 quart or larger bowl and at least six inches higher than the top of your bowl. In the top install an electric light socket and wire it up to a plug so that it can be plugged into an outlet.

Experiment with light bulbs of low wattage until you find the one which will keep the temperature at or near 85 degrees F. This will probably be a 7½ watt bulb. If this is too hot drill some ventilation holes in the side of the box. After you have found the right temperature just plug it in when you want to do some proofing.

An inexpensive proofing box is a styrofoam chest measuring about 12″ by 18″ which costs about $2.00 in most supermarkets and drugstores. Cut a hole in the top and insert an electric light socket through it. Fasten it securely and make sure that all electrical connections are properly covered so that there are no exposed wires or other parts to cause accidental shocks. A 7½ watt bulb will keep the inside at 85 degrees perfectly while allowing your kitchen to remain comfortable. This great idea comes from Mrs. Eileen Howard of San Lorenzo, California.

There are many other methods of achieving this temperature. A word of warning, however. Do not expose your sourdough starter or anything being made from your sourdough starter to direct heat source such as a range top, pilot light, a heater or even a powerful light bulb or heat lamp at close range. Remember that your proofing area should also be draft free, so don't use the top of a forced air heater or similar area to achieve this necessary temperature.

Many materials are useful in cooking and baking with sourdough. However, some do not withstand the high acidity of sourdough well and may cause contamination. Because of this we recommend that when storing your sourdough starter you use a 2 cup or larger plastic or stoneware container or a glass container specifically designed for sourdough as you can watch it work slowly over long periods of time. A regular glass jar is hazardous as it may crack or shatter under the pressure of the gases generated by the starter. It should be avoided, since this might happen even in the refrigerator.

A stoneware crock is one of the traditional containers for sourdough. It has the added glamour of tradition and thus proves to be a decorative as well as a practical container.

A plastic container of the type food products are sold is ideal. It is lightweight and easy to handle. Be sure that it is properly labeled to prevent others from inadvertently discarding your starter.

Any storage container should have some space at the top to prevent spillage when the starter is active and expands.

When setting a batter (see Chapter 4) always use a glass, stoneware or plastic bowl. Never leave the sourdough in contact with metal for a prolonged period of time. The authors also recommend that when stirring or mixing you use wooden or plastic spoons. Aluminum, especially cast aluminum, is to be avoided, as well as copper. Both may cause a drastic reduction in the purity and taste of your sourdough. Stainless steel bowls, utensils and beaters are fine for mixing your sourdough.

It is quite important to use bowls and pans of the size specified in the recipes. Sourdough is quite a powerful leavener and at times will cause your batter or dough to double or triple in size. Although this expanded size may be only temporary it is necessary to contain the batter or dough at its largest size. Failure to use large enough bowls can cause the mixture to overflow, which proves to be messy and quite difficult to clean up . A bristle vegetable brush and a plastic mesh ball aid tremendously in all phases of cleaning up after using sourdough.

The baking pans which you use will cause variation in the color and texture of your breads. Glass has the greatest heat absorbing qualities and thus needs less temperature than metal pans. All the temperatures for baking the recipes in this book were arrived at by using metal pans. If you are using a glass pan, reduce the temperature called for in the recipes by about 25 degrees.

Even at this lower temperature you will find that glass pans will give your breads the thickest crust. A shiny metal pan will cause a thin crust light in color. Lightweight aluminum causes the thinnest crust of all. Dark teflon will cause crust on the sides and bottom to be darker than when using any other type of pan.

TECHNIQUES

Baking bread with your sourdough starter is quite easy. There is an orderly method of baking bread which, if followed, will result in delicious bread. There are eight basic steps involved. Some are repeated once or twice during the process. These are stated below and discussed in detail in the following pages.

1. Preparation of Ingredients (Primary Batter)
2. Mixing the Primary Batter (see Chapter 4)
3. Setting the Batter (see Chapter 4)
4. Preparation of Ingredients
5. Mixing the Ingredients
6. Kneading the Dough
7. Rising or Proofing
8. Punching Down
9. Rising
10. Forming the Loaf
11. Rising
12. Baking

Not all steps are performed for every recipe. You will find a complete description of the steps needed with each recipe. This discussion is to make you aware of the role these steps play and to instruct you on how to perform these steps.

PREPARATION OF INGREDIENTS

Sourdough is very sensitive to temperature. It is essential that you bring all ingredients to room temperature before beginning to work with them. It is especially important to do this with the liquid ingredients such as water or milk. If you have stored your flour where it is cool or cold, let that come to room temperature also. If these items are not warm the action of the sourdough is retarded and all the rising or proofing periods will be extended. The proper temperature for any water added to a mixture is body temperature. The best method of testing if the water is at this temperature is to put a few drops on the inside of your wrist. It should not feel hot or cold. If it feels hot then let the water cool and if it feels cold then heat the water. The same is true for milk. When adding milk you may wish to scald it before using to insure that it is free of harmful bacteria. This is not really necessary with modern pasteurized milk, however. Eggs should also be allowed to come to room temperature before adding to the mixture.

Kneading the dough

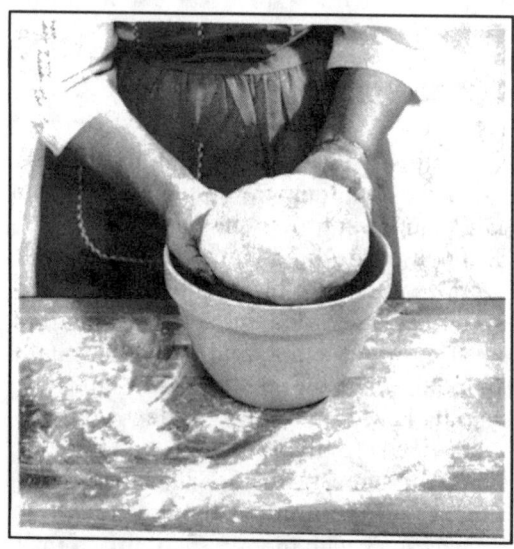

Placing dough in bowl for rising

Finger test for "double in bulk"

Forming the loaf

Pinching to seal

Placing dough in pan

MIXING THE INGREDIENTS

Mixing the ingredients should be done in a large bowl. The ingredients should be added in the order specified in the directions of each recipe. You will find that while flour is one of the first ingredients added, it also is one of the last in almost all cases. Flour should be added in small amounts of not more than ½ cup at a time. After each ½ cup of flour the batter should be well stirred.

KNEADING THE DOUGH

Kneading is the most critical step in the bread baking process. It is also the step in which the greatest amount of personal judgement is necessary. Dough which is ready for kneading should be turned out of the bowl onto a lightly floured bread or pastry cloth. Lightly floured means approximately a quarter cup of flour.

Kneading accomplishes two ends. It incorporates exactly the amount of flour necessary to bring the dough to the proper consistency to make the best bread and it structures the dough so that the leavening action of the sourdough starter is greatest.

It should be noted that the proper consistency of the dough is reached by kneading in any where from a tiny amount to several cups of flour. It is **not** kneading in as much flour as possible. Some doughs are sticky and soft before and after kneading. That is the way they are supposed to be and to knead in as much flour as possible will only cause your bread to be a heavy lump. Don't be afraid to get your hands just a little sticky while kneading. The sourdough will not hurt them. If you wish to prevent too much dough from sticking to your hands a light coating with cooking oil or butter will help.

The other aim of the kneading is to structure the elements of the dough in a manner which allows the gases produced by the sourdough to be most efficiently trapped and expanded when baked. This action provides the final lightness and texture of your bread. Kneading should be done in a rhythmical and orderly fashion to best structure the dough.

To knead, fold the dough towards you, then press the heel of your hand firmly into the dough. Rotate the dough one-quarter turn and then fold it towards you again and press the heel of your hand into it once more. Repeat this process rhythmically until the dough becomes smooth, elastic and satiny. As the flour on the board becomes absorbed into the dough keep sprinkling more flour onto the board. The amount of flour worked into the dough during the kneading process varies with the original moisture of the flour. This is the reason that bread recipes never have the exact amount of flour specified. After kneading, the dough should be placed in a greased bowl and turned over thus insuring that all sides of the dough receive a light coat of grease.

RISING

When the dough has been kneaded (or properly mixed for our no-knead breads) it needs a period of rest during which the sourdough can work. This period is called a proofing or rising time. As sourdough is very sensitive this proofing should be done in a draft free place which is kept as close to 85 degrees as possible. Methods of achieving this temperature have been discussed earlier in this chapter. There are two and sometimes three proofing periods associated with each bread making. During the initial proofing the dough is expected to "double in bulk" . This period is usually about two hours long. Its exact duration depends on many things including temperature and how well the bread was kneaded. This initial proofing is finished as soon as the imprint of two finger pushed about ½ inch into the dough remains. "Doubled in bulk" is an approximation. Use the finger test to find the proper time to continue with the recipe. At high altitudes this stage will be reached sooner than the two hour period.

Additional proofing periods vary in time but in all cases they are completed as soon as the imprint of the two fingers remains in the dough.

PUNCHING DOWN

This step is accomplished by pushing a fist directly and firmly into the center of the risen dough. Do this just once. Then fold the edges over into the impression and turn the dough over in the bowl.

FORMING THE LOAF

This step is dependent on the type of bread being baked. The common bread shape is that which is baked in a standard loaf pan. This type of loaf will be discussed at this time. The procedure for other breads will be described in the recipes for those types of bread.

When ready to shape the loaves pinch the dough into the same number of pieces as the number of loaves of bread that the recipe makes. Take a piece and throw it vigorously onto the board or pastry cloth. Using a rolling pin or the palm of your hand flatten it out until it is about one inch thick. Then roll the dough up into a cylindrical shape sealing it frequently by pinching the loaf to that which hasn't been rolled up yet. Pinch the final seam closed and using your hands press lightly on both ends of the loaf until it will just fit into the pan. Place the shaped loaf in the pan with the pinched edge down. The loaf should touch both ends of the pan to help it rise evenly during baking.

BAKING

The importance of a high quality oven thermometer has already been noted. The oven should be preheated to the temperature called for in the recipe. This heat should be achieved at least five minutes before putting the bread in the oven. Bread should be placed in the oven on the center rack or just slightly higher than center. Never crowd more than two loaves into the oven at the same time. Also, make sure that no pan is closer than two inches to another pan. For proper baking it is necessary that there be a free flow of air and heat around the pans.

To test for doneness check to see if the bread has shrunk away from the sides of the pan. This is the first indication that the bread is close to being done. To test further remove the pan from the oven and turn over, tapping to release the bread from the pan. Then tap the bottom of the loaf. If it sounds hollow the bread is done. When it is done, place the loaves on their sides on a wire rack to cool. Never let the bread cool in the pans or you will end up with soggy bread. Drafts while cooling will cause your bread to shrink.

There are a seemingly endless number of kinds of crust on breads. While each recipe has directions on the best way to achieve the type of crust the authors feel that is best suited to that bread, you may desire to have a different type of crust on your bread.

The section on utensils gives a description on how different types of pots and pans will change the color and consistency of your crust.

Crusts may also be made a darker brown if brushed before and during baking with milk. If you desire a hard, chewy crust brush the loaves with cold water just before placing them in the oven and twice during the first ten minutes of baking. A pan of boiling water in the bottom of the oven during the first ten minutes will also aid in developing a hard crust. A glazed crust can be achieved if the loaves are brushed with a mixture of one egg yolk mixed with 1 or 2 tablespoons of water or milk during the last few minutes of baking, A darker crust may be achieved by brushing your loaf twice during the final 15 minutes of baking with a mixture of 2 tablespoons of sugar in ¼ cup water.

STORAGE INFORMATION

Bread should be completely cooled before wrapping for storage to prevent the formation of mildew . The wrapping should be air tight if intended for freezing. For storage in a bread box or cupboard the bread should be allowed to breathe by leaving the end of the bag open or by punching holes in it.

CAKES

To make the best sourdough cakes be sure to stir the cake batter in one direction only. Do not reverse the direction in which you stir as it destroys the structure of the batter and will cause your cakes to rise unevenly.

TAKING YOUR SOURDOUGH CAMPING

If you are going camping and wish to take your sourdough starter along, there are no special precautions which must be taken. Depending on your mode of travel you will vary the method of carrying your sourdough starter into the wilds. By trailer, car or pack animal the starter can be carried directly as it comes from the refrigerator.

If you are backpacking, the best method of carrying your starter is to mix enough flour into it until it becomes a very soft ball. Place this ball in the center of the bag containing the rest of your flour. When you want to use it remove the ball of starter from the flour and thin it with warm water until it reaches the proper consistency for sourdough batter (see Chapter 4).

A reflector oven can produce as fine a quality baked bread as your oven at home and because of the fresh air it will taste even better. Bread may also be baked in a dutch oven type of kettle with great results and, of course, sourdough pancakes are the food that fed the miners in the days when they needed all their strength to pan for gold. Most of the recipes in this book can be used easily in camp cooking.

Chapter 3
Your Sourdough Starter

What is a sourdough starter? That is the first question people ask when the subject comes up. This chapter hopes to briefly answer this question and many others you may have about what sourdough starters are, how they work and what one does to keep them healthy for generations of good eating. Also included are directions on how to reactivate the sourdough starter from the Gold Rush Sourdough Company in a manner which will maximize all its great properties.

Sourdough starters have been with us since the time of the Egyptian Pharoahs. They have been important in European breads for centuries. A true sourdough starter has three initial ingredients — water, wheat flour, and the sourdough micro-organisms. These micro-organisms are alive and belong to the plant family. They are also related to the organisms which cause beer and wine to ferment, The original commercial yeast was extracted from hops which had been used in beer making. The sourdough feeds on the flour and water, growing and multiplying until it reaches a point at which it stabilizes. While growing fast it produces carbon dioxide gas as a by-product in the same manner that trees produce gases during the process of living and growing. It is these gases which cause bread to rise.

These micro-organisms known as Saccharomyces exiguus which are sourdough are a strain of acid loving species of yeast and a bacteria which scientists have named Lactobacillus San Francisco in honor of the fact that San Francisco bakeries continued to produce sourdough bread through those dark years when there was little awareness of good bread. With today's resurgent interest in good food value, gourmet cooking, and the emerging desire for better nutrition, many small bakeries all over the country are now producing sourdough bread.

An additional effect is that sourdough converts the carbohydrates in the endosperm of the wheat kernel into an alcoholic liquid. If a clear yellow liquid ever forms on the top of your starter this is nothing more than a very crude alcohol. The forty-niners and Alaskan Indians would imbibe this. However, it is a bit raw for modern taste. In fact, this is hooch named after an Alaskan Indian tribe which specialized in producing this sourdough liquor.

Sourdough causes your bread to rise because of the carbon dioxide gas given off by the sourdough trapped in the dough. When the gluten in the flour becomes wet it can stretch tremendously. The ability of the gluten to stretch is what keeps the gas bubbles trapped in the dough. Thus, the dough puffs up or, in other words, rises. This rising is what causes the lightness of sourdough and yeast breads compared with unleavened breads such as our forefathers' hearth cakes or ash cakes.

Sourdough also has an additional effect upon your bread since it imparts a tangy, nippy flavor to it. This gives the bread a definite character and provides a distinctive base against which all the other ingredients are highlighted.

The sourdough organisms are found all over the world. They are present in the air almost anywhere. For this reason many people advocate starting your own starter from scratch. There are hundreds of methods of starting a starter. Most of these involve mixing a liquid such as potato water or milk with flour and letting it set for several days. Some advocate using a commercial yeast. The former method is how the original starters began. Both are subject to many hazards. Perhaps the greatest one is that there are literally thousands of micro-organisms floating around in the air. Many of these are harmful, many more are of an unpleasant nature and while they leaven bread they will also give it a disagreeable taste. Therefore, a proven starter culture is the best place to get your starter from. This may be from a friend or neighbor who will give you a part of their starter or from a reputable source which will sell you a starter from a thoroughly proven master starter.

Your Gold Rush Sourdough Starter is a collection of completely natural organisms. No chemicals have been involved in its preparation. It never needs chemical preservatives, yet it will last you a lifetime with proper care. This care has been summarized in a list of do's and don'ts at the end of this chapter. The best type of care you can give your starter is to treat it as well as you would your favorite pet or house plant.

The proper place to store your starter is in the refrigerator on the bottom shelf. The low temperature slows down the activity of the starter. This serves to prevent the starter from eating all the flour and then dying due to a lack of food, and from becoming so sour that it overpowers all the other tastes in your bread.

This brings us to the point of discussing methods of controlling the sourness of your baked products. Many people are interested in bread with a stronger or weaker sourdough flavor than their starter naturally produces. The healthiest and strongest sourdough flavor comes from a starter which is used frequently. For a more sour result the best method is to let your Primary Batter (see Chapter 4) rest for more than the recommended twelve hour proofing period. A second method is to store your starter between uses in a warmer place than your refrigerator — a cool shelf in your cupboards, for example.

For a more mild sourdough flavor let the twelve hour proofing period of your Primary Batter be shortened. Never reduce it to less than six hours or you will not get the proper leavening action. This will result in heavy bread. Another method is to increase the amount of sugar in the bread by one tablespoon. A third method is to add ½ teaspoon of baking soda to the bread recipe. The authors prefer to keep their starters pure and do not add anything other than flour and water to them. However, the most drastic method of reducing the sourness of your bread is to stir ½ teaspoon of baking soda directly into your starter. This should not be done more than once a month at the risk of killing your starter.

For sourdough enthusiasts who need a larger starter, the following procedure is recommended. Place your starter in a large warm bowl. Add equal parts of warm and white flour to it until the mixture is the size of the desired starter. Stir this batter vigorously, cover it and set in a warm 85 degree spot for 8 to 10 hours. The result is an expanded starter which you treat and use in exactly the same manner as the original. Return it to the refrigerator in an adequately large container.

If at any time one-quarter or more of the total bulk of your starter is the clear yellow liquid on the top, it is time to stir well and throw half of the starter away. Replace that which you have thrown away with enough warm water and flour in equal parts to bring your starter up to its original level.

The most important aspect of care of sourdough starters is temperature. The sourdough starter is most active around 85 degrees F. As the temperature drops it becomes less and less active. At around 38 degrees F., your sourdough starter is only slightly active. This is the best temperature if you only use your starter periodically, such as two or three times a month.

If you don't plan to use your starter for several months, a good method of storage is freezing. Your sourdough starter can withstand several freezings and thawings during its lifetime. When thawing, let your sourdough starter come to room temperature gradually. Do not try to hasten its thawing by application of direct heat.

Never allow your starter to be exposed to heat above 95 degrees F. Temperatures above 95 degrees are very likely to kill your sourdough starter. In addition, these higher temperatures are also favorable to the growth of less pleasant micro-organisms. The result could be the death of your starter by such a malevolent organism. The necessity of never exposing your starter to such high temperatures is the most important safeguard you can take to insure preservation of your sourdough starter.

If your interest in certain types of food precludes the use of white flour (even that of the unbleached variety) you may wish to have a whole wheat, rye, or buckwheat starter. This is possible purely by substituting whole wheat, rye, or buckwheat flour for white flour when mixing up the starter from its dehydrated form. You may also produce such a sourdough starter by taking ¼ cup of a white flour starter and mixing it with 1½ cups of warm water and 2 cups of whole wheat, rye, or buckwheat flour. This mixture should be covered with plastic wrap and allowed to remain in a warm 85 degree spot for 24 hours.

TO PREPARE STARTER

Place the contents of your "Old Fashioned Sourdough Starter" packet from the Gold Rush Sourdough Company in a warm plastic, glass or stoneware bowl of about 1 quart capacity. Add 1¾ cup of white flour and stir in 1½ cups of warm water. Stir well with a plastic or wooden spoon until the mixture is smooth and lump free, An egg beater will also work well at this point as it also incorporates air. Cover the bowl with plastic wrap and set the bowl in a warm, 85 degree, draft free place for 24 hours. Stir your starter at least twice during this period. It will be slightly thinner after the twenty-four hour period is up. Let your starter rest in the refrigerator for 24 hours before attempting to use it.

After the 24 hour proofing your starter will have reached its normal strength. It will have a yeasty smell that sometimes reminds one of beer. Normally there may be a bit of clear fluid on the top. If the plastic wrap wasn't sealed well there may also be a crust. Just stir either back into the starter. Now your starter is ready for use. If you don't plan to use your starter now, place it in your starter container and place on the lower shelf of your refrigerator.

AN IMPORTANT WORD ABOUT WATER AND YOUR SOURDOUGH STARTER

We have found that tap water from municipal water supplies has large amounts of chemicals added for purification. These fluorides and chlorine compounds retard the effectiveness of, and sometimes even kill the sourdough. For best results we suggest that you use bottled water in mixing up your starter, in all primary batters and where water is called for in each recipe to insure that your sourdough masterpieces are light and tasty.

Assemble ingredients

Combine flour and starter

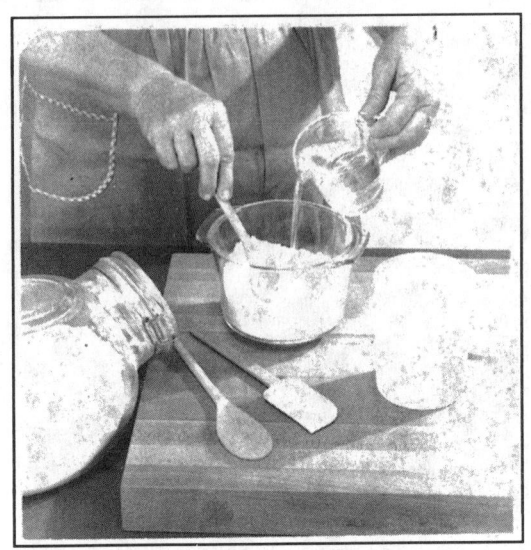

Add water to flour and starter mixture

Close container and label

REMEMBER

1. Use only wooden or plastic mixing spoons.
2. Use glass, plastic or stoneware bowls. Do not use copper or aluminum.
3. Use a stoneware, plastic or properly designed glass container in the refrigerator. A sealed glass jar is hazardous as the glass may crack or shatter.
4. Let all ingredients come to room temperature.
5. Do not try to hurry the proofing or rising by raising the temperature higher than 85 degrees F.
6. Use the inside of your wrist for determining the proper temperature of warm water to be added.
7. Do not ever allow your starter to be subject to a temperature above 95 degrees F. or it may die.
8. A WARM PLACE MEANS 85 DEGREES F. AND DRAFT FREE.
9. Remember that a clear yellow liquid may rise to the top of your starter. This is normal, just stir it back in.
10. Throughout its lifetime your sourdough starter may bubble and foam. This is normal.
11. Never add anything other than flour and water to your starter or you risk killing it or changing its characteristics drastically.
12. Label your starter container in the refrigerator. Because of its sour odor many have been thrown away by helpful souls cleaning out their friends' or family's refrigerator.

Chapter 4
Primary Batters & Room
Temperature Sourdough Starters

Primary Batter is basic to many of the recipes in this book. It is the mixture of your sourdough starter with warm water and flour which has set in a warm place for a twelve hour period. It is during this period that the sourdough multiplies itself. When the proofing period is over your batter will have the power to leaven your breads and rolls.

Primary Batters are used in many recipes in this book. The recipes given in this chapter for Primary Batters are the ones intended to be followed in this book. However, since each person has a very highly developed sense of what type of ingredients and handling should go into his food, we give suggestions on how to modify your Primary Batters to bring you a baked product which embodies your own concepts of food.

PRIMARY BATTER "A"

The recipe for Primary Batter "A" yields a greater amount of Primary Batter and is used for most of the bread and cake recipes in this book.

Ingredients
    1 cup sourdough starter
    2½ cups white flour
    2 cups warm water

Yield:
    3 cups Primary Batter "A" for baking
    1 cup batter to return to your starter container
    4 cups total.

PRIMARY BATTER "B"

The recipe for Primary Batter "B" is used for pancakes, rolls, muffins and biscuits.

Ingredients:
   1 cup sourdough starter
   1½ cups white flour
   1 cup warm water

Yield:
   1½ cups Primary Batter "B" for baking
   1cup batter to return to your starter container
   2½ cups total

1. Assemble all ingredients and utensils.

2. Remove your sourdough starter from the refrigerator and stir it well. Take out one cup and place it in a warm bowl of 2 quart or larger capacity. Return the remaining starter to the refrigerator. The large size bowl is necessary to prevent spillage as the batter will expand greatly during its proofing period. The final quantity will be around the 2½ or 4 cups total.

3. Add the warm water and stir until well mixed. Slowly add the white flour stirring continually to blend the flour in well. Stir 4 to 5 minutes or until the mixture is smooth and lump free, or use an egg beater or electric mixer.

4. Cover the bowl with plastic wrap and place it in a warm draft free area for proofing.

5. The proofing period is 8 to 12 hours depending on how active your starter is when taken from the refrigerator. Your batter is ready when it is foamy and full of large bubbles and can be used at any time after this point up to 4 hours. If your batter has many tiny bubbles in it, it has already reached the proper state. If few or no bubbles are present during the 8 to 12 hours after proofing, your starter is not acting properly and you should determine the reason for this before continuing with the recipe.

6. During the proofing period there is a chance that crust will form on the top of your batter. If this happens just stir it back down into the batter. The same is true of any liquid which might form on the top.

7. At the end of the proofing period stir the batter thoroughly. Take out one cup and put it back into your starter container. Stir your starter thoroughly and return it to your refrigerator.

ROOM TEMPERATURE SOURDOUGH STARTER

This is an alternative to the procedure of preparing a batter 8 to 12 hours before you intend to start a recipe. It is designed only for those recipes which call for it either directly or as an alternate to the Primary Batter. The use of sourdough starter rather than a primary batter in the other recipes will cause failures.

The proper procedure to prepare your Room Temperature Sourdough Starter is as follows:

1. Remove your sourdough starter from the refrigerator and measure out the amount of starter called for in the recipe. Set this in a warm 85 degree spot for 1 hour.

2. Add enough warm water and white flour in equal parts to the remaining starter to bring it back up to its original level in its storage container. Stir it well and return it to the refrigerator.

If the recipe calls for more than half of your starter and you desire to use your starter within the next week, it is recommended that the replenished starter be placed in a warm 85 degree spot for 8 to 12 hours before returning it to the refrigerator in order to restore its strength.

One cup starter

Add starter to flour and water

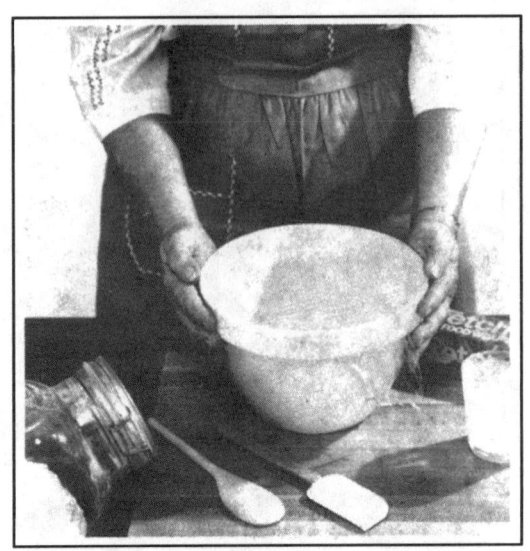

Cover and place in 85 degree area

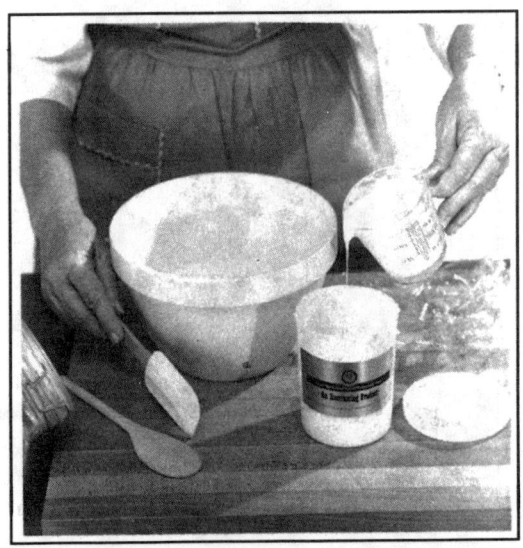

Return one cup to starter

Many people do not want 30 pancakes or two loaves of bread at a time. Many recipes in this book are scaled for that amount. If you desire less, any recipe in the book may be halved. However, halving a recipe may cause the amount of flour which must be added during the kneading process or during the final stirring for no-knead breads and pancakes to be different. Therefore, when halving a bread recipe, be sure to add the flour slowly at the end so that you stop when the proper texture is reached. If halving a pancake or waffle recipe, be sure that when adding the major liquid ingredient that you add it a little at a time until the proper texture of batter is reached.

For larger quantities than those made by these recipes there are inherent risks in doubling. This is particularly true for breads and cakes. The pancake and waffle recipes can be doubled with no trouble other than being careful when adding the major liquid ingredient. Not as much of this liquid will be needed for large quantities. Add only as much as you feel will bring the texture of the pancake batter to the same as that in the standard recipe. If you wish to bake larger quantities of breads or cakes it is recommended that you double the Primary Batter recipe but after returning the proper amount to your starter and that you divide the remainder of the batter into two parts of three cups each. Proceed from there as if you were making the same recipe twice. This requires more bowls, etc., but will insure that you will be baking high quality loaves of bread and cakes.

If you are using a starter of buckwheat, whole wheat, or other non-white flour, substitute whatever flour you are using for the white flour in either Primary Batter recipe. This may cause your batter to be slightly thicker than with white flour but will not harm or hinder the proper working of your sourdough starter. The use of a whole grain flour may necessitate increasing the 12 hour proofing period. Experiment and see whether you feel that an extended period is desirable.

A final word about sourdough cooking and baking is in order at this point. Pancakes and waffles are the easiest recipes in this book. It is for this reason that they are first. Therefore, we recommend that you begin with one of these recipes. Your first adventure into bread baking, particularly if you are a beginner, should be the no-knead white bread recipe, the first recipe in Chapter 6.

Having read these first four chapters, you are now ready to embark upon your sourdough adventure.

Chapter 5
Pancakes & Waffles

Pancakes, griddle cakes, flapjacks, johnny cakes or whatever you may call them are America's oldest form of bread. Originally pancakes were nothing more than ground grain (corn or wheat) and water baked on hot stones. As pancakes developed some form of leavening was added to provide lightness.

Mankind has developed pancakes wherever he has lived. Most cultures have their special type of pancake. Some are simple, some fancy. Some are breakfast cakes and some are dessert pancakes. America's version is the sourdough pancake.

PANCAKES

First, a word or two about pancakes and how to make them. Pancakes may be cooked on almost any type of hot surface. This surface can be an electric griddle, electric fry pan, ordinary fry pan or an aluminum or cast iron griddle placed over a flame. All produce fine pancakes. For each type of utensil the manufacturer's directions for seasoning should be followed. In fact, the authors prefer to season all their pots and pans when new whether necessary or not, and periodically thereafter to provide a smooth nonsticking cooking surface and to prolong the useful life of the utensils.

For cooking pancakes it is advisable to first take a small amount of butter or cooking oil and rub it into the cooking surface of the utensil. For cast iron and aluminum pans you may find it desirable to do this between each batch of pancakes.

Heat your pan to 375-400 degrees temperature. The proper temperature is specified with each recipe. A rough test of the correct temperature is where a few drops of cold water will bounce and dance on the pan. If they immediately turn to steam the temperature is too hot. If they lie there the temperature is too cold. Be sure that your pan reaches the correct temperature at least five minutes before actually cooking the pancakes.

Pancakes should be cooked by carefully ladling or spooning the pancake batter directly onto the pan. A tablespoon produces pancakes of silver dollar size. These are the authors' favorites. A quarter cup measure will produce a 4-5 inch pancake.

Pancakes should cook for 3-4 minutes on the first side. They are ready to be turned when bubbles are evenly distributed over the top surface and the edges begin to dry. At this time the bottom should be nicely browned. This can be checked by carefully lifting the edge of one and looking at it. When they reach this degree of doneness flip them over and cook on the second side for about half as long as the first side. The second side does not brown as evenly as the first. For pancakes larger than silver dollar size, the cooking time is slightly longer.

Ideally, pancakes should be served directly from the pan onto the plate. They are most delicious at this time. However, if you want to cook up enough for everyone, keep the cooked pancakes in a 225-250 degree oven in a covered container.

The syrup served with pancakes or waffles should be warm for the best taste. The end of this chapter has several recipes for different and exciting syrups which can be served with pancakes and waffles.

Your sourdough pancakes will have a different texture than the pancakes you are used to because the batter has set for 12 hours. Ordinary pancakes are cooked immediately after mixing. Because the gluten in this flour has had a chance to become elastic over the proofing period of the Primary Batter your sourdough pancakes will have a firmer texture. This should be expected.

Many people prefer sourdough pancakes which are even firmer. To achieve this omit ¼ cup of flour from the recipe. This will give you traditional, thin, firm sourdough pancakes.

Sometimes you will have pancake batter left over. It doesn't keep very well in batter form. To avoid wasting batter, cook it up into pancakes or waffles. Let them cool, then stack them with a piece of wax paper or plastic wrap between each one. Place them in an airtight plastic bag or other container and freeze them. They will keep up to two weeks in the freezer. They can be gradually thawed and then reheated in butter in a frying pan or put in a covered baking dish in a 375 degree oven until warmed through.

Many things can be done with pancakes. Don't let the standard form and use of pancakes limit your imagination. Unsweetened pancakes and waffles make wonderful bases for all those dinner and lunch dishes for which you usually use rice, mashed potatoes or bread. Regular pancakes can be made into interesting shapes by creative pouring of the batter onto the griddle. Greased cookie cutters can be placed on the griddle and batter poured into them. This will give your pancakes all the interesting shapes your cookie cutters have. Children love these pancakes. For a wide variety of different tastes don't hesitate to experiment with different types of flour and with all sorts of fresh fruit and diced meats. We have included many suggestions on how to vary your pancakes with little effort.

SOURDOUGH PANCAKES

For your first experience in your sourdough adventure we recommend sourdough pancakes because of their good taste with very little effort and their assurance of mouth watering success.

> 1½ cups Primary Batter "B"
> ½ cup white flour
> 1 egg
> 1 TBS sugar
> 1 TBS melted butter
> ¾ tsp salt
> 2 TBS milk

Yield: About 20 small pancakes.

1. Prepare the Primary Batter "B" following the directions in Chapter 4. Be sure that you have returned 1 cup of the batter to your sourdough starter container before proceeding with the recipe.

2. Assemble all ingredients and utensils. Let all ingredients come to room temperature. This is important if you wish to avoid tough rubbery pancakes.

3. Place the 1½ cups of Primary Batter "B" in a warm bowl. Add the ½ cup of white flour. Beat the egg lightly and stir it into the batter. Stir in the 1 TBS of sugar.

4. Add the 1 TBS of melted butter and the ¾ tsp of salt.

5. Stir in the 2 TBS of milk.

6. Heat your griddle to 400 degrees as described in the section at the beginning of this chapter. When the griddle is heated, ladle batter directly onto the cooking surface with a serving spoon or pour from a mixing cup. The best tasting sourdough pancakes are approximately 2 inches in diameter.

7. In 3-4 minutes the top will be covered with bubbles and the edges will begin to dry. If the undersides are browned, then turn them and cook on the other side. The second side cooks in about half the time the first side took and tends not to brown as evenly.

8. Serve immediately with butter and warmed syrup or other topping of your choice. We find that many of the fruit and berry toppings now available enhance the flavor of your sourdough pancakes.

GRANDMA BOYD'S SOURDOUGH PANCAKES

This recipe comes from the kitchen of Grandma Boyd. It is her favorite recipe for sourdough pancakes.

> 1½ cups Primary Batter "B"
> ½ cup white flour
> 1 egg
> 2 TBS melted butter
> ¼ cup instant dry milk
> 1 tsp salt
> 2 TBS sugar

Yield. about 20 small pancakes.

1. Prepare Primary Batter "B" following the directions in Chapter 4. Be sure that you have returned one cup of the batter to your sourdough starter container in the refrigerator.

2. Assemble all ingredients and utensils. Let all ingredients come to room temperature.

3. Place the 1½ cups of Primary Batter "B" in a warmed bowl. Add the ½ cup of white flour.

4. Beat the egg until light and frothy and stir it into the batter,

5. Stir in the 2 TBS of melted butter and the ¼ cup of instant dry milk.

6. Sift the 1tsp of salt and the 2 TBS of sugar over the mixture and fold it in. Let the batter rest 15-20 minutes.

7 . Spoon or ladle the batter onto a preheated 400 degree griddle in small amounts.

8. When the top is full of bubbles and the bottom is browned (about 3-4 minutes) turn the pancakes and cook on the other side for 1½-2 minutes.

9. Serve them hot with butter and warm syrup or other topping of your choice.

Note: If you desire lighter pancakes, fold ¼ tsp of baking soda dissolved in 1tsp of water into the batter with the salt and sugar.

SOURDOUGH BUTTERMILK PANCAKES

1½ cups Primary Batter "B"
2 eggs
2 TBS sugar
2 TBS melted butter
1½ tsp salt
1 cup buttermilk
1½ cups white flour
Yield: about 25 2-inch pancakes.

1. Prepare the Primary Batter "B" following the directions in Chapter 4. Before mixing in the other ingredients be sure that you have returned the cup of batter to your sourdough starter storage container in the refrigerator.

2. Assemble all ingredients and utensils. Let all ingredients come to room temperature.

3. Put the 1½ cups of Primary Batter "B" in a warm bowl.

4. Beat the eggs slightly and stir them into the batter.

5. Stir in the 2 TBS of sugar, the 2 TBS of melted butter and 1½ tsp of salt.

6. Stir in the 1 cup of buttermilk.

7. Stir in the 1½ cups of white flour. The batter may be lumpy. Let the batter rest in a warm place for 20 minutes.

8. Onto a preheated, 400 degree griddle (use drops of cold water to test for proper temperature) spoon or ladle out the batter in small amounts.

9. When the top is full of bubbles and the bottom is browned (about 3-4 minutes) turn each pancake and cook it for another 1½-2 minutes or until the second side is browned.

10. Serve hot with butter and warm syrup or other topping of your choice.

Note. If you desire pancakes which are lighter, fold in ¼ tsp of baking soda dissolved in 1tsp of water into the batter just after adding the 1½ cups of white flour.

SOURDOUGH SOUR CREAM PANCAKES

1½ cups Primary Batter "B"
1 cup sour cream
1 cup white flour
2 eggs
2 TBS sugar
2 TBS melted butter
1½ tsp salt

Yield: about 20 small pancakes.

1. Prepare the Primary Batter "B" following the directions in Chapter 4. Before adding any other ingredients be sure that you have returned 1cup of the batter to your sourdough starter container.

2. Assemble all ingredients and utensils. Let all ingredients come to room temperature.

3. Put the 1½ cups of Primary Batter "B" in a warm bowl. Stir in the 1 cup of sour cream. Add ½ cup of white flour.

4. Beat the 2 eggs and stir them into the batter.

5. Stir in the 2 TBS of sugar, the 2 TBS of melted butter and the 1½ tsp of salt.

6. Stir in the remaining ½ cup of white flour. The batter may be lumpy. Let it rest for 15-20 minutes.

7. Spoon or ladle the batter onto a preheated griddle at 400 degrees in small amounts.

8. In 3-4 minutes when the edges begin to dry and the top is full of bubbles, turn the pancakes and cook them for 1½-2 minutes on the second side.

9. Serve them hot with butter and the topping of your choice.

Note: If you desire lighter pancakes, fold ¼ tsp of baking soda dissolved in 1 tsp of water into the batter after adding the flour.

SOURDOUGH WHOLE WHEAT PANCAKES I

1½ cups Primary Batter "B"
2 eggs
2 TBS sugar
2 TBS melted butter
1½ tsp salt
½ cup milk
1¼ cups whole wheat flour
Yield: about 15 2-inch pancakes.

1. Prepare the 1½ cups of Primary Batter "B" following the directions in Chapter 4. Before mixing the other ingredients in, be sure that you have returned one cup of your batter to your sourdough starter container.

2. Assemble all ingredients and utensils. Let all ingredients come to room temperature.

3. Put the 1½ cups of Primary Batter "B" in a warm bowl.

4. Beat the eggs and stir them into the batter.

5. Stir in the 2 TBS of sugar, the 2 TBS of melted butter, and the 1½ tsp of salt.

6. Stir in the ½ cup of milk.

7. Stir in the 1¼ cups of whole wheat flour. Let the batter rest for 15-20 minutes.

8. Spoon or ladle the batter onto a preheated 400 degree griddle in small amounts.

9. When the tops are full of bubbles and the bottoms are browned (about 3-4 minutes), turn the pancakes and let them cook on the other side for 1½-2 minutes.

10. Serve them hot with butter and the topping of your choice.

Note: If you desire lighter pancakes, fold ¼ tsp of baking soda dissolved in 1 tsp of water into the batter just after adding the 1 cup of whole wheat flour.

SOURDOUGH WHOLE WHEAT PANCAKES II

This recipe is for those who have a whole wheat starter. It makes whole wheat pancakes with no white flour at all. This gives them a distinctly different and more hearty flavor.

> 1½ cups Primary Batter "B" (made with whole wheat flour)
> ¼ cup milk
> 1 egg
> 2 tsp sugar
> 2 TBS melted butter
> 1 tsp salt
> 1 cup whole wheat flour

Yield: about 20 small pancakes.

1. Prepare the Primary Batter "B" following the directions in Chapter 4. Be sure that you use whole wheat flour rather than white flour. Before mixing any other ingredients into your batter be sure that you have returned 1 cup of the batter to your whole wheat sourdough starter.

2. Assemble all ingredients and utensils. Let all ingredients come to room temperature.

3. Put the 1½ cups of Primary Batter "B" in a warm bowl. Stir in the ¼ cup of milk.

4. Beat the eggs and stir them into the batter.

5. Stir in the 2 tsp of sugar, the 2 TBS of melted butter and the 1 tsp of salt.

6. Stir in the 1 cup of whole wheat flour. The batter may be lumpy. Let it rest for 15-20 minutes.

7. Spoon or ladle the batter onto a preheated griddle at 400 degrees in small amounts.

8. When the tops are full of bubbles and the bottoms are browned, turn the pancakes and let them cook on the other side for about half the time they cooked on the first side.

9. Serve them hot with butter and the topping of your choice.

Note: For lighter pancakes fold ¼ tsp of baking soda dissolved in 1 tsp of water into the batter after adding the 1 cup of whole wheat flour. If you substitute 1cup of white flour for the 1 cup of whole wheat flour you will also get much lighter pancakes.

SOURDOUGH BUCKWHEAT PANCAKES I

1½ cups Primary Batter "B"
2 eggs
2 TBS sugar
2 TBS melted butter
1½ tsp salt
1 cup milk
1 cup buckwheat flour
Yield: about 15 2-inch pancakes.

1 . Prepare the Primary Batter "B" following the directions in Chapter 4. Before mixing other ingredients in be sure that you have returned one cup of the batter to your sourdough starter container.

2. Assemble all ingredients and utensils. Let all ingredients come to room temperature.

3. Put the 1½ cups of Primary Batter "B" in a warm bowl.

4. Beat the eggs slightly and stir them into the batter.

5. Stir in the 2 TBS of sugar, the 2 TBS of melted butter and the 1½ tsp of salt.

6. Stir in the 1 cup of milk.

7. Stir in the 1 cup of buckwheat flour. Let the batter rest for 15-20 minutes.

8 . Spoon or ladle the batter onto a preheated 400 degree griddle in small amounts.

9. When the top is full of bubbles and the bottom is browned (about 3-4 minutes) turn the pancakes and let them cook on the other side for 1½-2 minutes.

10. Serve them hot with warm molasses or other topping.

SOURDOUGH BUCKWHEAT PANCAKES II

This recipe is for those who have buckwheat starters. It makes pancakes with a very strong buckwheat flavor.

> 1½ cups Primary Batter "B"
> ¼ cup milk
> 1 egg
> 2 TBS sugar
> 2 TBS melted butter
> 1 tsp salt

Yield: about 20 small pancakes.

1. Prepare the Primary Batter "B" following the directions in Chapter 4. Be sure that you use buckwheat flour rather than white flour when making up the batter. Before mixing in other ingredients be sure that you have returned one cup of the batter to your buckwheat sourdough starter.

2. Assemble all ingredients and utensils. Let all ingredients come to room temperature.

3. Put the 1½ cups of buckwheat Primary Batter "B" in a warm bowl. Stir in the ¼ cup of milk.

4. Beat the egg and stir it into the batter.

5. Stir in the 2 TBS of sugar, the 2 TBS of melted butter, and the 1 tsp of salt.

6. Spoon or ladle the batter onto a preheated griddle at 400 degrees in small amounts.

7. When the top is full of bubbles and the bottom is browned (about 3-4 minutes), turn the pancakes and let them cook on the second side for 1½-2 minutes.

8. Serve them hot with butter and warm syrup or other topping.

Note: If you desire lighter pancakes, fold ¼ tsp of baking soda dissolved in 1 tsp of water into the batter just before cooking. Addition of ½ cup of white flour just before cooking will result in lighter pancakes. No other adjustments are necessary.

SOURDOUGH RYE PANCAKES I

This recipe produces exceptionally delicious pancakes.

1½ cups Primary Batter "B"
½ cup milk
2 eggs
2 TBS wheat germ
2 TBS melted butter
¼ cup molasses
1½ tsp salt
1 cup rye flour

Yield: about 20 small pancakes.

1. Prepare the 1½ cups of Primary Batter "B" following the directions in Chapter 4. Be sure that you have returned 1 cup of the batter to your sourdough starter container before adding other ingredients.

2. Assemble all ingredients and utensils. Let all ingredients come to room temperature.

3. Put the 1½ cups of Primary Batter "B" in a warm bowl. Stir in the ½ cup of milk.

4. Beat the 2 eggs and stir them into the batter.

5. Stir in the 2 TBS of wheat germ, the 2 TBS of melted butter, the ¼ cup of molasses, and the 1½ tsp of salt.

6. Stir in the 1 cup of rye flour. Let the batter rest for 15-20 minutes.

7. Spoon or ladle the batter onto a preheated 375 degree griddle in small amounts.

8. When the top is full of bubbles and the bottom is brown in about 3-4 minutes, turn the pancakes and let them cook for another 1½-2 minutes on the other side.

9. Serve them hot with butter and molasses or other topping.

Note: If you desire lighter pancakes, fold ¼ tsp of baking soda dissolved in 1 tsp of water into the batter just after adding the 1 cup of rye flour.

SOURDOUGH RYE PANCAKES II

This recipe is for those who have a rye starter. It produces rye pancakes with a more definite rye taste than the first recipe.

    1½ cups Primary Batter "B" (made with rye flour)
    ¼ cup milk
    1 egg
    ¼ cup molasses
    2 TBS melted butter
    1 tsp salt
Yield: about 20 small pancakes.

1. Prepare the Primary Batter "B" using rye flour for the white as directed in Chapter 4. Be sure that you have returned 1 cup of the batter to your rye sourdough starter before proceeding with recipe.

2. Assemble all ingredients and utensils. Let all ingredients come to room temperature.

3. Put the 1½ cups of rye Primary Batter "B" in a warm bowl. Stir in the ¼ cup of milk.

4. Beat the egg and stir it into the batter.

5. Stir in the ¼ cup of molasses, the 2 TBS of melted butter, and the 1 tsp of salt into the batter.

6. Spoon or ladle the batter onto a preheated griddle at 375 degrees in small amounts.

7. After 3-4 minutes the edges will begin to dry and the tops will be full of bubbles. If the bottoms are browned, turn the pancakes and cook them for an additional 1½-2 minutes.

8. Serve them hot with butter and syrup or other topping.

Note: If you desire lighter pancakes, fold ¼ tsp of baking soda dissolved in 1 tsp of water into the batter just before cooking. The addition of ½ cup of white flour stirred into the batter before cooking will also cause your pancakes to be lighter.

SOURDOUGH BANNOCKS (OATCAKES)

1½ cups of Primary Batter "B"
2 eggs
2 TBS sugar
2 TBS melted butter
1½ tsp salt
1 cup milk
1 cup rolled oats
Yield: about 20 2-inch pancakes.

1. Prepare the 1½ cups of Primary Batter "B" following the directions in Chapter 4. Before mixing in other ingredients be sure that you have returned one cup of your batter to your sourdough starter container.

2. Assemble all ingredients and utensils. Let all ingredients come to room temperature.

3. Put the 1½ cups of Primary Batter "B" in a warm bowl.

4. Beat the two eggs and stir them into the batter.

5. Stir in the 2 TBS sugar, the 2 TBS melted butter, and the 1½ tsp of salt.

6. Stir in the 1 cup of milk.

7. Stir in the 1 cup of rolled oats. The batter may be lumpy. Let it rest for 15-20 minutes.

8. Spoon or ladle the batter onto a preheated 400 degree griddle in small amounts.

9. When the top is full of bubbles and the bottom is browned (about 3-4 minutes) turn the pancakes and let them cook on the other side for 1½-2 minutes.

10. Serve them hot with butter and the syrup of your choice.

Note: If you desire lighter pancakes fold ¼ tsp of baking soda dissolved in 1 tsp of water into the batter just after adding the 1 cup of rolled oats.

SOURDOUGH CORNMEAL PANCAKES

1½ cups Primary Batter "B"
2 eggs
2 TBS sugar
2 TBS melted butter
1½ tsp salt
½ cup milk
1 cup yellow cornmeal
Yield: about 15 2-inch pancakes.

1. Prepare the 1½ cups of Primary Batter "B" following the directions in Chapter 4. Before mixing in other ingredients be sure that you have returned one cup of your batter to your sourdough starter container.

2. Assemble all utensils and ingredients. Let all ingredients come to room temperature.

3. Put the 1½ cups of Primary Batter "B" in a warm bowl.

4. Beat the eggs and stir them into the batter.

5. Stir in the 2 TBS sugar, the 2 TBS of melted butter, and the 1½ tsp of salt.

6. Stir in the ½ cup of milk.

7. Stir in the 1 cup of yellow cornmeal. Let the batter rest for 15-20 minutes.

8 . Spoon or ladle the batter onto a preheated 400 degree griddle in small amounts.

9. When the top is full of bubbles and the bottom is browned turn the pancakes. Let them cook for 1½-2 minutes on the second side.

10. Serve them with butter and the topping of your choice.

Note: If you desire lighter pancakes, fold ¼ tsp of baking soda dissolved in 1 tsp of water into the batter just after adding the cornmeal.

SOURDOUGH RYE CORNMEAL PANCAKES

    1½ cups Primary Batter "B"
    ½ cup milk
    2 eggs
    ¼ cup molasses
    2 TBS melted butter
    1½ tsp salt
    ½ cup cornmeal
    ½ cup rye flour
Yield. about 20 small pancakes.

1 . Prepare the Primary Batter "B" following the directions in Chapter 4. Be sure that you have returned one cup of batter to your sourdough starter container before adding other ingredients.

2. Assemble all ingredients and utensils. Let all ingredients come to room temperature.

3. Place the 1½ cups of Primary Batter "B" in a warm bowl. Stir in the ½ cup of milk.

4. Beat the 2 eggs and stir them into the batter.

5. Stir in the ¼ cup of molasses, the 2 TBS of melted butter and the 1½ tsp of salt.

6. Stir in the ½ cup of cornmeal and the ½ cup of rye flour. The batter may be lumpy. Let it rest for 15-20 minutes.

7. Spoon or ladle the batter onto a preheated 375 degree griddle in small amounts.

8. When the tops are full of bubbles and the bottoms are browned turn the pancakes and let them cook on the other side for about half the time that the first side took.

9. Serve hot with butter and the topping of your choice.

Note: If you desire lighter pancakes, fold ¼ tsp baking soda dissolved in 1 tsp of water into the batter after stirring in the rye flour.

SOURDOUGH WHOLE WHEAT
YOGURT PANCAKES

1½ cups Primary Batter "B"
½ cup yogurt
2 eggs
2 TBS sugar
2 TBS melted butter
1½ tsp salt
1 cup whole wheat flour
Yield: about 20 small pancakes.

1. Prepare the Primary Batter "B" following the directions in Chapter 4. Before mixing in other ingredients be sure that you have returned 1 cup of your batter to your sourdough starter container.

2. Assemble all ingredients and utensils. Let all ingredients come to room temperature.

3. Put the 1½ cups of Primary Batter "B" in a warm bowl. Stir in the ½ cup of yogurt.

4. Beat the two eggs and stir them into the batter.

5. Stir in the 2 TBS of sugar, the 2 TBS of melted butter, and the 1½ tsp of salt.

6. Stir in the 1 cup of whole wheat flour. The batter may be lumpy. Let it rest for 15-20 minutes.

7. Spoon or ladle the batter onto a preheated 400 degree griddle in small amounts.

8. When the tops are full of bubbles and the bottoms are browned in approximately 3-4 minutes, turn the pancakes and let them cook on the other side for 1½-2 minutes longer.

9. Serve them with the topping of your choice. Honey is a particularly good topping for these pancakes.

Note: If you desire lighter pancakes, fold ¼ tsp baking soda dissolved in 1 tsp of water into the batter just after adding the 1 cup of whole wheat flour.

SOURDOUGH SQUASH PANCAKES

1 cup Room Temperature Sourdough Starter
1 egg
1 TBS sugar
1 TBS melted butter
1 tsp salt
½-¾ cup mashed cooked squash
¼ cup white flour
Yield: about 25 small pancakes.

1. Prepare the Room Temperature Sourdough Starter following the directions in Chapter 4. Be sure to replenish your original starter before proceeding with the recipe.

2. Assemble all ingredients and utensils. Let all ingredients come to room temperature.

3. Place the 1 cup of sourdough starter at room temperature in a 1 quart or larger bowl. Beat 1 egg and stir it and 1 TBS sugar into the starter.

4. Melt 1 TBS butter and stir it and 1 tsp salt into the batter.

5. Mash enough cooked squash to make ½ to ¾ cup and stir it into the batter. Stir in ¼ cup of white flour.

6. Spoon or ladle the batter onto a preheated 375 degree griddle.

7. When the top is full of bubbles and the bottom is browned (about 3-4 minutes) turn the pancakes and cook on the other side for 2-3 minutes longer.

8. Serve hot with molasses or the topping of your choice.

Note: For lighter, larger pancakes add ½ tsp baking soda when you add the sugar.

SOURDOUGH SOUR CREAM GRAHAM PANCAKES

This recipe produces exceptionally delicious pancakes.

1½ cups Primary Batter"B"
1 cup sour cream
2 eggs
2 TBS sugar
2 TBS melted butter
1½ tsp salt
1 cup graham flour
Yield: about 20 small pancakes.

1. Prepare the 1½ cups of Primary Batter "B" following the directions in Chapter 4. Be sure that you have returned 1cup of the batter to your sourdough starter container before adding any other ingredients.

2. Assemble all ingredients and utensils. Let all ingredients come to room temperature.

3. Put the 1½ cups of Primary Batter "B" in a warm bowl. Stir in the 1 cup of sour cream.

4. Beat the two eggs and stir them into the batter.

5. Stir in the 2 TBS of sugar, the 2 TBS of melted butter and the 1½ tsp of salt.

6. Stir in the 1 cup of graham flour. The batter may be lumpy. Let is rest for 15-20 minutes.

7. Spoon or ladle the batter onto a preheated 400 degree griddle in small amounts.

8 . When the bottoms are browned in about 3-4 minutes turn the pancakes and let them cook on the other side for 1½-2 minutes longer.

9. Serve them hot with whipped honey butter or other topping of your choice.

SOURDOUGH BAKED FRUIT PANCAKES

1½ cups Primary Batter "B"
6 eggs
¼ cup sugar
¼ cup butter
½ tsp salt
½ pint sour cream
1½ cups drained fruit (sliced apples, peaches, bananas or
        strawberries are good but you can use any fruit you
        happen to have handy)
¼ cup lemon juice
1 tsp vanilla
Yield: 7-8 servings.

1. Prepare the 1½ cups of Primary Batter "B" following the directions in Chapter 4. Before mixing in other ingredients be sure that you have returned one cup of your batter to your sourdough starter container.

2. Assemble all ingredients and utensils. Let all ingredients come to room temperature.

3. Put the 1½ cups of Primary Batter "B" in a warm 2 quart or larger bowl.

4. Separate each egg. Beat the yolks slightly and stir them into the batter.

5. Stir in the ¼ cup sugar, the ¼ cup of melted butter, and the ½ tsp salt.

6. Stir in the 1 tsp of vanilla, the ¼ cup of lemon juice, and the ½ pint of sour cream.

7. Beat the egg whites until they are fluffy. Fold the egg whites and the fruit into the batter.

8. Pour into 2 greased 9-inch round pans and place in a preheated 375 degree oven for 20 minutes. It is done when the top has browned.

Other Types of Pancakes

The basic pancake recipe, the first one in this chapter, lends itself well to many variations. The standard procedure for creating new and exciting types of pancakes with this basic recipe is to stir in the ingredient which makes the pancake different the very last thing. This added ingredient can make a world of difference to those who are becoming tired of the same type of pancakes day after day, but at the same time causes only a very little extra effort on the part of the cook. The ingredients which can be added to pancakes generally fall into two classes. These are the fruit ingredients and the meat ingredients. Fruits can completely change the nature of your pancakes. Fresh fruits or canned ones may be used. For a more hearty type of pancake diced or chopped meats will give your pancakes a robust and hearty flavor.

Sourdough Apple Pancakes

Use the basic Sourdough Pancake recipe at the beginning of this chapter. After adding the milk, stir in 1 cup of sliced apples, which have been sprinkled with ¼ tsp baking soda dissolved in hot water, 1 tsp nutmeg and 1 tsp vanilla. Cook the pancakes as directed. Serve with hot honey.

Sourdough Banana Pancakes

Use the basic Sourdough Pancake recipe at the beginning of the Chapter. After adding the milk stir in 1 cup of mashed or sliced bananas and ¼ tsp baking soda which has been dissolved in 1 tsp water. Cook as directed. Serve with butter and honey.

Sourdough Blueberry Pancakes

Use the basic Sourdough Pancake recipe at the beginning of the chapter. After adding the milk add 1 cup of fresh or well-drained canned or frozen blueberries, ¼ tsp baking soda, and 4 additional TBS of sugar to the batter. Stir well and cook as directed. Serve topped with butter and fresh blueberries in blueberry sauce.

Sourdough Sour Cream Blueberry Pancakes

Use the Sour Cream Sourdough Pancake recipe and after adding the sour cream add ¾ cup of fresh or well-drained canned or frozen blueberries and 2 TBS additional sugar. Stir well and cook as directed. Serve with butter.

Sourdough Pineapple Pancakes

Use the basic Sourdough Pancake recipe at the beginning of this chapter and after adding the milk, stir in one cup of drained crushed pineapple and ¼ tsp of baking soda dissolved in 1 tsp water. Cook as directed. Serve with butter and a sprinkling of brown sugar.

Sourdough Strawberry Pancakes

Use the basic Sourdough Pancake recipe at the beginning of this chapter and after adding the milk stir in one cup of fresh crushed strawberries and ¼ tsp of baking soda dissolved in 1 tsp water. Cook as directed. Serve with whipped cream and a topping of whole fresh strawberries. Alternately starting with the basic Sourdough Pancake recipe at the beginning of this chapter, stir in 1 cup of frozen strawberries which have been thawed. Cook as directed and serve with a topping of strawberry syrup.

Sourdough Ham Pancakes

Follow the basic Sourdough Pancake recipe at the beginning of this chapter. After adding the milk stir in 1 cup of diced ham. Cook as directed and serve with butter.

Sourdough Shrimp Pancakes

Follow the basic Sourdough Pancake recipe at the beginning of this chapter. After adding the milk stir in the contents of a 1-ounce can of cocktail shrimp. Cook as directed. Serve with butter.

Sourdough Frankfurter Pancakes

Follow the basic Sourdough Pancake recipe at the beginning of this chapter. After adding the milk stir in two finely diced frankfurters. Cook as directed. Serve hot with butter.

Sourdough Bacon Pancakes

Follow the basic Sourdough Pancake recipe at the beginning of this chapter. After adding the milk add 6-8 slices of bacon which have been fried and finely crumbled. Cook as directed and serve with butter.

Sourdough Corn Pancakes

Follow the basic Sourdough Pancake recipe at the beginning of this chapter. After adding the milk add the contents of a well-drained 12-ounce can of whole kernel corn. Stir well and cook as directed. Serve hot with butter.

Sourdough Rice Pancakes

Follow the basic Sourdough Pancake recipe at the beginning of this chapter. After adding the milk stir in ½ cup cooked rice and ½ tsp vanilla. Cook as directed and serve hot with butter.

Sourdough Cornflake Pancakes

Follow the basic Sourdough Pancake recipe at the beginning of this chapter. After adding the milk stir in 1 cup of cornflakes and cook as directed. Serve hot with butter and maple syrup or other topping.

Sourdough Peanut Butter Pancakes

Follow the basic Sourdough Pancake recipe at the beginning of this chapter. Omit the butter and add in its place ½ cup of melted peanut butter. After adding the milk add 6-8 slices of fried bacon which have been finely crumbled. Cook as directed. Serve hot.

Sourdough Beer Pancakes

Follow the basic recipe for Sourdough Pancakes at the beginning of this chapter. Instead of adding milk, add ¼ cup of beer. It can be either fresh or stale beer as there will be no difference in the taste. This is a great way to make use of that half bottle of beer which has been sitting in the refrigerator for a week. Cook as directed and serve hot with butter and your favorite topping.

Waffles

Waffles have a very close kinship to pancakes. Because of this fact you can convert the pancake recipes to waffle recipes (excluding the baked pancakes) with little trouble. Waffles can be made on an electric waffle iron or in the old fashioned type of waffle iron which was placed over the flame. Follow the manufacturer's directions for care and seasoning of your waffle iron. It should then give you many years of service.

Waffles should be baked on a preheated surface. Therefore let your waffle iron come to its cooking temperature a few minutes before starting to bake your waffles. Electric waffle irons usually indicate when they are ready. The temperature needed for sourdough waffles is about 25 degrees higher than that used for ordinary waffles.

In general approximately ½ cup of batter will be the correct amount for a 6-inch square waffle iron. Pour this amount of batter onto the griddle when hot and let it spread evenly over the entire surface. Close the cover. When steam stops issuing from the waffle iron which generally takes around 6-7 minutes the waffle should be done. Lift the top and see if the waffle is nicely browned. If it is then remove it and serve it immediately. If it has not browned properly close the lid and let it bake for approximately 1 minute more.

Waffle irons do not generally need to be greased. The normal waffle batter has a considerable amount of butter or cooking oil which serves to keep the waffles from sticking. This amount of butter may seem quite rich but it is also what gives your waffles their crispy texture so it is not advisable to try to reduce the amount in the recipes. Remember also that unless served immediately your waffles will have a tendency to wilt. For this reason waffles which are intended for use as a base for other foods should generally contain much less sugar as it is the sugar which causes the wilting. Do not stack waffles as this also causes them to wilt.

Waffles may be frozen and reheated by using the same procedures as for pancakes. In addition, because of their rigid texture they can also be thawed by putting them in a toaster until heated through.

The pancake recipes can be adapted for use as waffle recipes by using the following steps. The amount of butter in each recipe should be doubled and the amount of sweeteners halved. The egg(s) should be separated and the yolk added instead of the whole egg(s) and the white(s) should be beaten until they form peaks and then gently folded into the batter as the last step before baking. Using this procedure you can bake delicious waffles using the pancake recipes already given. There are also some additional waffle recipes given in the following pages to give you an even wider choice.

SOURDOUGH WAFFLES

1½ cups Primary Batter "B"
2 eggs separated
2 tsp sugar
1 tsp salt
¼ cup melted butter
¼ cup milk
Yield 5 6-inch square waffles.

1. Prepare the Primary Batter "B" following the directions in Chapter 4. Be sure that you have returned 1 cup of the batter to your sourdough starter container before proceeding with the recipe.

2. Assemble all ingredients and utensils. Let all ingredients come to room temperature.

3. Put the 1½ cups of Primary Batter "B" in a warm bowl.

4. Separate the eggs. Beat the egg yolks lightly and stir them into the batter.

5. Stir the 2 tsp of sugar and the 1 tsp of salt into the batter.

6. Stir the ¼ cup of melted butter and the ¼ cup of milk into the batter.

7. Beat the egg whites until they form soft peaks. Fold them gently into the batter.

8. Pour the batter onto a preheated waffle iron. The iron should be slightly hotter than when baking regular waffles. The batter should be thin enough that when the iron is closed it spreads out to cover the entire surface of the iron. Close the top.

9. After about 6 minutes when no more steam is coming from the waffle iron lift the top. If the waffles are a golden brown they are done. If they are not yet done close the top and let them bake for an additional minute.

10. When done, serve the waffles hot. Because of the large amount of butter in the waffles they do not need buttering. Just top them with maple syrup, honey, whipped cream, ice cream, or other topping.

SOURDOUGH BUTTERMILK WAFFLES

1½ cups Primary Batter "B"
2 eggs separated
2 tsp sugar
1 tsp salt
¼ cup butter
¼ cup buttermilk
Yield: 5 6-inch square waffles.

1. Prepare the 1½ cups of Primary Batter "B" according to the directions in Chapter 4. Before mixing in the other ingredients be sure that you have returned one cup of the batter to your sourdough starter container.

2. Assemble all ingredients and utensils. Let all ingredients come to room temperature.

3. Put the 1½ cups of Primary Batter "B" into a warm 2-quart or larger bowl.

4. Separate the eggs. Beat the egg yolks lightly and stir them into the batter. Stir in the 2 tsp sugar and the 1 tsp salt.

5. Melt the butter and stir it and the ¼ cup of buttermilk into the batter.

6. Beat the egg whites until they form soft peaks. Gently fold them into the batter.

7. Pour batter onto a preheated waffle iron. The batter should spread out and cover the surface of the iron. Close the top.

8. After about 6 minutes when no more steam is coming from the waffle iron lift the top. If the waffles are a golden brown they are done. If they are not done close the top and let them cook for another minute.

9. When done remove from the waffle iron and serve immediately.

SOURDOUGH WHOLE WHEAT WAFFLES I

1½ cups Primary Batter "B"
½ cup milk
2 eggs separated
2 tsp sugar
1 tsp salt
¼ cup melted butter
½ cup whole wheat flour

Yield: 5 6-inch square waffles.

1. Prepare the 1½ cups Primary Batter "B" following the directions in Chapter 4. Be sure that you have returned 1 cup of the batter to your sourdough starter container before proceeding with the recipe.

2. Assemble all ingredients and utensils. Let all ingredients come to room temperature.

3. Put the 1½ cups of Primary Batter "B" in a warm bowl. Stir in the ½ cup of milk.

4. Separate the eggs. Beat the egg yolks lightly and stir them into the batter.

5. Stir in the 2 tsp of sugar, the 1 tsp of salt, and the ¼ cup of melted butter.

6. Stir in the ½ cup of whole wheat flour a small amount at a time.

7. Beat the egg whites until they form soft peaks. Gently fold them into the batter. This batter will be thinner than that for the basic waffles.

8. Pour enough batter onto the waffle iron to evenly fill all the crevices in the iron. Do not use anything to spread the batter around after it has been poured, however, or you will lose some of the crispy texture of the waffles. Close the top.

9. After about 6 minutes and when steam stops coming out of the waffle iron, lift the top and check to see if the waffle is a golden brown. If it is it is done and it should be removed from the iron and served immediately. If not done close the top for approximately another minute.

SOURDOUGH WHOLE WHEAT WAFFLES II

This recipe is for those who have a whole wheat starter.

> 1½ cups Primary Batter "B" (made with whole wheat flour)
> 2 eggs separated
> 1 tsp salt
> 2 tsp honey
> ¼ cup melted butter
> ¼ cup milk

Yield: 5 6-inch square waffles.

1. Prepare the 1½ cups of Primary Batter "B" according to the directions in Chapter 4. Use whole wheat flour instead of white flour. Be sure that you have returned one cup of your batter to your whole wheat sourdough starter container before mixing in other ingredients.

2. Assemble all ingredients and utensils. Let all ingredients come to room temperature.

3. Put the 1½ cups of Primary Batter "B" into a warm 2-quart or larger bowl.

4. Separate the eggs. Beat the egg yolks lightly and stir them into the batter. Stir in the 1 tsp of salt.

5. Stir in the 2 tsp honey, the ¼ cup of melted butter and the ¼ cup of milk.

6. Beat the egg whites until they form soft peaks. Gently fold them into the batter.

7. Pour about ½ cup of the batter onto a preheated 6-inch waffle iron. Close the top.

8. After about 6 minutes and when no more steam is coming from the waffle iron, lift the top and if the waffles are a golden brown they are done. If they are not yet done close the top and let them cook for another minute.

9. Remove the waffles from the waffle iron and serve them hot.

SOURDOUGH CORNMEAL WAFFLES

1½ cups Primary Batter "B"
3 eggs separated
2 tsp sugar
1 tsp salt
¼ cup butter
½ cup milk
¾ cup cornmeal

Yield: 5 6-inch square waffles.

1 . Prepare the 1½ cups of Primary Batter "B" according to the directions in Chapter 4. Before mixing in the other ingredients be sure that you have returned one cup of the batter to your sourdough starter container.

2. Assemble all ingredients and utensils. Let all ingredients come to room temperature.

3. Put the 1½ cups of Primary Batter "B" into a warm 2-quart bowl.

4. Separate the eggs. Beat the egg yolks lightly and stir them into the batter. Stir in the 2 tsp of sugar and the 1 tsp of salt.

5. Melt the butter and stir it and the ½ cup of milk and cornmeal into the batter.

6. Beat the egg whites until they form soft peaks. Gently fold them into the batter.

7. Pour about ½ cup of the batter onto a 6-inch preheated waffle iron. The batter should spread out enough to cover the entire surface of the iron. Close the top.

8. After 4 minutes and when no more steam is coming from the waffle iron lift the top. If the waffles are a golden brown they are done. If they are not done close the top and let them cook for another minute.

9. When done remove them from the iron and serve them immediately.

HELEN'S SOURDOUGH SOUR CREAM WAFFLES

      1½ cups Primary Batter "B"
      2 eggs
      2 tsp sugar
      1 tsp salt
      1 cup sour cream
Yield: 5 6-inch square waffles.

1. Prepare the Primary Batter "B" following the directions in Chapter 4. Be sure that you have returned 1 cup of batter to your sourdough starter container before proceeding with recipe.

2. Assemble all ingredients and utensils. Let all ingredients come to room temperature.

3. Put the 1½ cups of Primary Batter "B" in a warm bowl.

4. Separate the eggs. Lightly beat the yolks and stir them into the batter. Stir in the 2 tsp sugar and the 1 tsp salt.

5. Stir in the 1 cup of sour cream.

6. Beat the egg whites until they form soft peaks and gently fold them into the batter.

7. Pour the batter onto a preheated waffle iron. Close the top.

8. After about 7 minutes and when steam stops coming out of the waffle iron lift the top and if the waffles are a golden brown they are done. If not yet done close the top and let them cook for about 1 minute more.

9. Remove them from the waffle iron and serve them hot.

SOURDOUGH GOLDEN YAM WAFFLES

1½ cups Primary Batter "B"
2 eggs separated
2 tsp sugar
1 tsp salt
¼ cup butter
¼ cup milk
½-¾ cup boiled mashed yams
Yield: 5 6-inch square waffles.

1 . Prepare the 1½ cups of Primary Batter "B" according to the directions in Chapter 4. Before mixing in the other ingredients be sure that you have returned one cup of the batter to your sourdough starter container.

2. Assemble all ingredients and utensils. Let all ingredients come to room temperature.

3. Put the 1½ cups of Primary Batter "B" into a warm 2-quart bowl.

4. Separate the eggs. Beat the egg yolks lightly and stir them into the batter. Stir in the 2 tsp of sugar and the 1 tsp of salt.

5. Melt the butter and stir it, the ¼ cup of milk, and the yams into the batter.

6. Beat the egg whites until they form soft peaks. Gently fold them into the batter.

7. Pour batter onto a preheated waffle iron. The batter should spread out enough to cover the entire surface of the iron. Close the top.

8. After about 6 minutes and when no more steam is coming from the waffle iron, lift the top. If the waffles are a golden brown they are done. If they are not done, close the top and let them cook for another minute.

9. When done, remove them from the iron and serve them immediately.

SOURDOUGH GINGERBREAD WAFFLES

1½ cups Primary Batter "B"
2 eggs separated
½ cup white flour
2 TBS brown sugar
1 tsp cinnamon
1 tsp ginger
¼ tsp allspice
1 tsp salt
¼ cup butter
2 TBS molasses
½ cup milk
Yield: 5 6-inch square waffles.

1. Prepare the 1½ cups of Primary Batter "B" according to the directions in Chapter 4. Before mixing in the other ingredients be sure that you have returned one cup of the batter to your sourdough starter container.

2. Assemble all ingredients and utensils. Let all ingredients come to room temperature.

3. Put the 1½ cups of Primary Batter "B" in a warm 2-quart bowl.

4. Separate the eggs. Beat the egg yolks slightly and stir them into the batter.

5. Stir in the ½ cup of flour, the 2 TBS of firmly packed brown sugar, the 1 tsp of cinnamon, the 1 tsp of ginger, the ¼ tsp of allspice and the 1 tsp of salt.

6. Melt the butter and stir it into the batter. Stir in the 2 TBS of molasses and the ½ cup of milk.

7. Beat the egg whites until they form soft peaks. Gently fold them into the batter.

8. Pour about ½ cup of the batter onto a preheated 6-inch waffle iron. The batter should spread out to cover the entire surface of the iron. Close the top.

9. After about 7 minutes and when no more steam is coming from the waffle iron, lift the top. If the waffles are a golden brown they are done. If they are not yet done close the top and let them cook for another minute.

10. When done remove them from the iron and serve them topped with vanilla ice cream.

SOURDOUGH BRANDY PECAN WAFFLES

1½ cups Primary Batter "B"
2 eggs separated
2 tsp sugar
1 tsp salt
¼ cup butter
¼ cup milk
½ cup finely chopped pecans
2 TBS brandy
Yield: 5 6-inch square waffles.

1 . Prepare the 1½ cups of Primary Batter "B" according to the directions in Chapter 4. Before mixing in the other ingredients be sure that you have returned one cup of the batter to your sourdough starter container.

2. Assemble all ingredients and utensils. Let all ingredients come to room temperature.

3. Put the 1½ cups of Primary Batter "B" into a warm 2-quart bowl.

4. Separate the eggs. Beat the egg yolks lightly and stir them into the batter. Stir in the 2 tsp of sugar and the 1 tsp of salt.

5. Melt the butter and stir it and the 2 TBS of brandy into the batter.

6. Stir in the ½ cup of finely chopped pecans and the ¼ cup of milk.

7. Beat the egg whites until they form soft peaks. Gently fold them into the batter.

8. Pour the batter onto a preheated waffle iron. The batter should spread out to cover the entire surface of the iron. Close the top.

9. After about 6 minutes and when no more steam is coming from the waffle iron, lift the top. If the waffles are a golden brown they are done. If they are not yet done close the top and let them cook for another minute.

10. When done remove them from the iron and serve them immediately.

SOURDOUGH CHOCOLATE DESSERT WAFFLES

1½ cups Primary Batter "B"
2 eggs separated
3 TBS sugar
¾ tsp salt
½ cup cocoa
½ tsp vanilla
¼ cup butter
¾ cup milk

Yield: 5 6-inch square waffles.

1. Prepare the 1½ cups of Primary Batter "B" according to the directions in Chapter 4. Before mixing in the other ingredients be sure that you have returned one cup of the batter to your sourdough starter container.

2. Assemble all ingredients and utensils. Let all ingredients come to room temperature.

3. Put the 1½ cups of Primary Batter "B" in a warm 2-quart bowl.

4. Separate the eggs. Beat the egg yolks lightly and stir them into the batter. Stir in the 3 TBS of sugar, the ¾ tsp of salt, the ½ cup of cocoa and the ½ tsp vanilla.

5. Melt the butter and stir it and the ¾ cup of milk into the batter.

6. Beat the egg whites until they form soft peaks and gently fold them into the batter. This batter is thinner than for other types of waffles.

7. Pour batter onto a preheated waffle iron. The batter should spread out enough to cover the entire surface of the iron. Close the top.

8. After 7 minutes and when no more steam is coming from the waffle iron lift the top. If the waffles are a dark brown they are done. If they are not yet done close the top and let them cook for another minute.

9. When they are done remove these delicious cake-like waffles from the iron and serve them with whipped cream, ice cream or vanilla pudding.

Waffle Variations

Waffles are just as easily adapted to variations of flavor and texture as are pancakes. There is a seemingly endless number of these variations as there are with pancakes. You are urged to experiment with the variations suggested for pancakes in your waffle baking. We are sure that you will receive as many compliments and as much praise as we have when we have served these delicious variations to our friends.

Syrups and Garnishes

Pancakes and waffles are ideally suited to a topping which will complement their taste and perhaps also bring an additional flavor into play. The most common topping is maple syrup and butter. This is so traditional that many times we just do not think to try something different. Currently there are a great variety of syrups and toppings available from the local supermarket. In addition, there are also a great number of syrups and toppings which can be made from fresh fruit, canned or frozen fruit, and the many spices and extracts available today. Following are some that the authors feel well suited for pancakes and waffles.

Orange Syrup

    1 cup maple syrup
    1 tsp frozen orange juice concentrate
    2 TBS butter

Heat the above ingredients in a small saucepan until all are soft and can be stirred together. Serve hot with pancakes or waffles. Especially suited for wholewheat pancakes or waffles.

Spicy Orange Syrup

    1 cup maple syrup
    1 tsp frozen orange juice concentrate
    1 tsp prepared mustard
    1/8 tsp ground cloves
    2 TBS butter

Heat all ingredients over a low flame until soft. Stir them together and serve hot on pancakes or waffles.

Honey Topping I

    1 cup honey
    1 tsp cinnamon
    ½ tsp nutmeg
    ¼ tsp allspice
Stir the spices into the honey and warm slightly.

Honey Topping II

    1 cup honey
    1½ tsp frozen juice concentrate
    2 tsp grated orange rind
Stir the frozen juice concentrate and the grated orange rind into the honey.

Honey Plum Topping

    1 cup pureed plums
    ½ cup honey
    ¼ tsp allspice
    ½ tsp nutmeg
Stir together all ingredients over a low flame. When all have been thoroughly mixed, serve as a topping for waffles.

Brown Sugar

    ½ cup brown sugar
    ½ cup butter
Melt the butter over a low flame and stir in the brown sugar in small amounts. When all the brown sugar has melted and has been stirred thoroughly into the butter the syrup is ready to be poured over the top of your pancakes and waffles.

Boiled Cider

    2 cups cider
    1 cup sugar
Stir the sugar into the cider and place over a flame. Boil the liquid down until it has thickened to a syrup. Stir it while it is thickening to prevent burning.

Peach Butter

½ cup butter
½ cup peach preserves
1/8 tsp nutmeg

Beat the three ingredients together. Serve as a topping to pancakes.

Blueberry Syrup

2 cups blueberries
½ cup sugar
½ cup water
slice of lemon

Simmer all ingredients together, stirring frequently to make a syrup.

Maple-Rum Syrup

1 cup maple syrup
½ cup butter
1 oz. Rum

Melt the butter and stir the maple syrup and Rum into it. Serve hot.

Hot Spiced Applesauce Topping

1 17-ounce can applesauce
½ tsp cinnamon
¼ cup firmly packed brown sugar

Stir all three ingredients together and heat. Serve hot on waffles. Makes a delicious topping for apple pancakes.

Praline Sauce

1 cup firmly packed brown sugar
½ cup corn syrup
¼ cup water
½ cup chopped pecans
2 TBS butter

Heat the first three ingredients together in a small sauce pan and when they have reduced to a syrup, stir in the ½ cup of chopped pecans and the 2 TBS of butter.

Hot Spiced Honey Butter

½ cup butter
½ tsp cinnamon
¼ tsp nutmeg
½ cup honey

Melt the butter over moderate heat. Stir in the remaining ingredients and serve while warm.

Other Toppings

An attractive and tasty topping is sour cream and your favorite variety of jam or jelly on your pancakes or waffles. Or you might try grating some semi-sweet chocolate on top of whipped cream. Butterscotch syrup is quite tasty on pancakes and waffles. Many people like the taste of molasses and corn syrup in the toppings they heap upon their pancakes. Cottage cheese is another favorite. The possibilities are endless.

Chapter 6
Appetizers & Crackers

This part of your sourdough adventure leads you into the realm of appetizers made from your sourdough starter. These are different and exciting treats due to the tangy base flavor imparted by the starter. In addition, the sourdough crackers are a delight to make and eat.

SOURDOUGH PRETZELS

This recipe produces those old time pretzels with the hard crust and a soft bread-like inside.

> 1½ cups Primary Batter "B"
> 1 cup hot water
> 2 TBS butter
> 3 TBS sugar
> 2 tsp salt
> 5½ cups flour
> 1 egg yolk
> 2 TBS thick cream or evaporated milk

Yield: 20 pretzels 4-5 inches across.

1. Prepare the Primary Batter "B" following the directions in Chapter 4. Be sure that you have returned 1 cup of the batter to your sourdough starter container.

2. Assemble all ingredients and utensils. Let all ingredients come to room temperature.

3. Add the 2 TBS butter, the 3 TBS sugar, and the 2 tsp salt to the 1 cup of hot water. Cool to lukewarm.

4. Put the 1½ cups of Primary Batter "B" in a warm bowl. Add the water mixture after it has cooled.

5. Add 4 cups of the flour, ½ cup at a time, stirring after each addition.

6. Turn out onto a floured board and knead in approximately 1½ cups more of the flour. The dough will be very stiff.

7. Place the dough in a greased bowl, turn over and cover. Let set for 2 hours to proof.

8. On a board which has been scraped clean of flour break off pieces of the dough about the size of large egg. Roll each piece out with the palms of your hands until it is about 18 inches long and ½ inch in diameter. Twist into the shape of a pretzel.

9. Place on a greased cookie tin. Brush them with egg yolk mixed with 2 TBS of heavy cream or evaporated milk. Cover and place in a warm 85 degree spot for 30 minutes for proofing.

10. After proofing, brush again with the egg and cream mixture and sprinkle with coarse salt.

11. Bake in a preheated 425 degree oven for 15 minutes. Remove and cool on wire racks.

SOURDOUGH BREAD STICKS

1½ cups Primary Batter "B"
1 cup hot water
2 TBS butter
3 TBS sugar
2 tsp salt
3¾-4 cups flour
Yield: about 40 bread sticks.

1 . Prepare the Primary Batter "B" following the directions in Chapter 4. Be sure that you have returned 1 cup of the batter to your sourdough starter container before proceeding with the recipe.

2. Assemble all ingredients and utensils. Let all ingredients come to room temperature.

3. Combine the hot water, the 2 TBS of butter and the 3 TBS of sugar and allow the mixture to cool to 90 degrees.

4. Put the 1½ cups of Primary Batter "B" in a warm bowl and stir in the cooled-hot water, butter and sugar liquid. Add the 2 tsp of salt and stir.

5. Add approximately 3 cups of flour ½ cup at a time to the batter.

6. When the dough is too stiff to stir, turn out onto a floured board and knead in enough additional flour (about ¾-1 cup) to make the dough smooth and elastic.

7. Place the dough in a greased bowl and cover. Let set in a warm 85 degree place for approximately 2 hours until the dough is doubled in bulk.

8. Divide the dough into two balls. Roll each ball out on a floured board to a thickness of ½ inch. Slice the dough into long strips about ½ inch wide.

9. Roll each strip with your hands on the floured board to make them cylindrical.

10. Brush them with water and place about 1 inch apart on a lightly greased baking sheet.

11 . Bake in a preheated 400 degree oven for 20 minutes or until brown.

SOURDOUGH BLINI

Blini are Russian pancakes usually served topped with sourcream and caviar. This treat has been adapted to sourdough cooking to provide you with an exciting addition to your culinary arts.

    1 cup Room Temperature Sourdough Starter
    1 TBS sugar
    ¼ cup evaporated milk
    2 eggs beaten
    1 tsp baking soda
    ½ tsp salt
    ½ cup flour
    2 TBS butter
Yield: about 18-20 Russian pancakes.

1. Prepare the Room Temperature Sourdough Starter following the directions in Chapter 4. Be sure to replenish your original starter before proceeding with the recipe.

2. Assemble all ingredients and utensils. Let all ingredients come to room temperature.

3. Put the 1 cup of sourdough starter in a 1 quart or larger bowl. Add 1 TBS sugar and ¼ cup evaporated milk. Stir well.

4. Beat the 2 eggs and stir them into the batter.

5. Stir in the 1 tsp baking soda, ½ tsp salt and ½ cup of white flour.

6. Cover the bowl and let rest in a warm 85 degree spot for 30 minutes.

7. Place the 2 TBS butter in a skillet and cook the batter as you would pancakes, turning once only. Small cakes are best, each made with slightly under ¼ cup of batter.

8. Serve with sour cream. If you are being really Russian serve with both sour cream and red caviar.

Note: Omit the salt if you are serving the blini with caviar.

SOURDOUGH SCONES

This adaptation of the Scottish scone is great when served warm with large amounts of butter and jelly. It is a good tea bread and a good breakfast bread.

> 1 cup Room Temperature Sourdough Starter
> 2 TBS sugar
> ½ tsp salt
> 1 tsp baking soda
> ¼ cup melted butter
> 1 egg beaten
> 1 cup white flour

Yield: 10-12 scones

1. Prepare the Room Temperature Sourdough Starter following the directions in Chapter 4. Be sure to replenish your original starter before proceeding with the recipe.

2. Assemble all ingredients and utensils. Let all ingredients come to room temperature.

3. Place the 1 cup of room temperature starter in a 1 quart or larger bowl. Stir in 2 TBS sugar, ½ tsp salt and 1 tsp baking soda.

4. Stir in ¼ cup of melted butter making sure that the butter is only melted but not hot.

5. Beat 1 egg and stir it into the batter.

6. Stir in 1 cup of flour. This should make a dough which can be dropped from a spoon.

7. Drop large serving spoonfuls of the batter into a greased frying pan over medium heat. Cook scones until brown on the bottom and then turn over and cook until brown on the second side.

8. Serve warm with lots of butter and jelly.

SOURDOUGH USZKA

Uszka are Polish ravioli type dough pockets filled with mushrooms and onions. These are great appetizers and also make a great addition to clear soups.

> 1 cup Room Temperature Sourdough Starter
> 1 tsp salt
> 1 cup white flour
> 2 TBS butter
> 1 chopped onion
> ½ pound chopped mushrooms
> ½ tsp pepper

Yield: about 24 filled dough pockets.

1. Prepare the Room Temperature Sourdough Starter following the directions in Chapter 4. Be sure to replenish your original starter before proceeding with the recipe.

2. Assemble all ingredients and utensils. Let all ingredients come to room temperature.

3. Add 1 tsp salt and 1 cup of white flour to the 1 cup of room temperature sourdough starter. Stir well and turn out onto a floured bread board.

4. Knead until smooth and form a large ball. Cover and set in a warm 85 degree spot for 30 minutes.

5. While the dough is proofing prepare the filling in the following manner.

6. Melt 2 TBS butter in a frying pan. Add 1 chopped onion, ½ pound chopped mushrooms and ½ tsp pepper and saute for 10 minutes. Then turn heat up high for 1 minute to evaporate any remaining water vapor. Stir continually to prevent burning.

7. Cool for 15 minutes.

8. Roll the dough out to a thickness of 1/8 inch. Cut it into 3 inch squares.

9. Place 1 TBS of filling on each square. Fold up the dough and pinch to seal. Let rest for 15 minutes.

10. Cook in boiling water with 2 tsp salt for 12 minutes. Serve on toothpicks with a sharp sauce. If desired to add to soups add just before serving if just cooked. If they have been allowed to cool add during the last 5 minutes of cooking.

SOURDOUGH SALT CRACKERS

These crispy salt crackers make a perfect accompaniment to soups and salads. In addition they are great with peanut butter and other spreads.

> ½ cup Room Temperature Sourdough Starter
> 2 TBS shortening
> 2 tsp salt
> 1 cup white flour

Yield: about 60 crackers.

1. Prepare the Room Temperature Sourdough Starter following the directions in Chapter 4. Be sure to replenish your original starter before proceeding with the recipe.

2. Assemble all ingredients and utensils. Let all ingredients come to room temperature.

3. Add 2 TBS shortening (melted) and 2 tsp salt to the ½ cup of starter. Stir in about ⅔ cup of the flour.

4. Turn out onto a highly floured (about ⅓ cup) board and knead thoroughly adding flour while kneading. This will take approximately ½ of the flour on the board.

5. When the dough is extremely stiff roll it out to a thickness of 1/16 inch.

6. Cut the dough with a sharp knife or a pizza cutter into 1 inch by 3 inch rectangles.

7. Place these on an ungreased cookie tin so they are slightly separated.

8. Prick each cracker several times with a fork. This must be done to prevent the crackers from puffing up.

9. Sprinkle with additional salt.

10. Bake in a 400 degree oven for 7 to 8 minutes or until the crackers start to brown slightly.

11. Cool thoroughly and store in an airtight container. If crackers become soggy place them in a 300 degree oven for about 5 minutes to restore crispness.

SOURDOUGH WHOLE WHEAT CRACKERS

A great treat when served spread with pineapple cheese.

1 cup Room Temperature Sourdough Starter
1 tsp dill
1 tsp salt
½ cup shortening
2 cups whole wheat flour
Yield: about 100 crackers.

1 . Prepare the Room Temperature Sourdough Starter following the directions in Chapter 4. Be sure to replenish your original starter before proceeding with the recipe.

2. Assemble all ingredients and utensils. Let all ingredients come to room temperature.

3. Place 2 cups of whole wheat flour in a warm bowl and add 1 tsp dill and 1 tsp salt. Cut in ½ cup of shortening until the mixture resembles coarse cornmeal.

4. Stir in 1 cup sourdough starter at room temperature. The dough should just hold together.

5. Turn the dough onto a whole wheat floured board and roll out to a thickness of 1/8 inch. Cut into 2 inch squares and place on greased cookie sheets. Prick with a fork to prevent puffing.

6. Bake in a preheated 375 degree oven for 25-30 minutes or until the crackers brown.

SOURDOUGH CORNMEAL CHEESE CRACKERS

These crackers are a natural with most dips.

½ cup Room Temperature Sourdough Starter
1 cup cornmeal
½-¾ cup white flour
½ tsp salt
½ cup shortening
⅓ cup grated Parmesan cheese
Poppy seeds
Yield: about 72 crackers

1. Prepare the Room Temperature Sourdough Starter following the directions in Chapter 4. Be sure to replenish your original starter before proceeding with the recipe.

2. Assemble all ingredients and utensils. Let all ingredients come to room temperature.

3. Cut the shortening into the cornmeal until it is the size of small peas.

4. Stir the ½ cup of sourdough starter into the cornmeal shortening mixture.

5. Stir in the ⅓ cup of Parmesan cheese, ½ cup white flour and ½ tsp salt. Turn the dough out onto a board floured with about ¼ cup flour.

6. Knead until the dough is stiff. It is a very crumbly dough. Roll the dough out to a thickness of 1/16 inch. Do not try to reroll any of the dough as it will be almost impossible to do so.

7. Cut the dough into 1 by 3 inch rectangles. Place the cut pieces on an ungreased cookie sheet and prick with a fork. Sprinkle with poppy seed.

8. Bake in a 350 degree oven for 12 minutes.

SOURDOUGH RYE THINS

1 cup Room Temperature Sourdough Starter
1 tsp salt
1 tsp rosemary
½ cup butter
2¼ cups rye flour
Yield: about 120 small rye crackers

1 . Prepare the Room Temperature Sourdough Starter following the directions in Chapter 4. Be sure to replenish your original starter before proceeding with the recipe.

2. Assemble all ingredients and utensils. Let all ingredients come to room temperature.

3. Place the 1 cup of sourdough starter in a warm bowl. Add 1 tsp salt and 1 tsp rosemary.

4. Stir in ½ cup melted butter and 2 cups rye flour ½ cup at a time, stirring well after each addition.

5. Put about ¼ cup rye flour on a board, turn the dough out onto it and knead a few times. Divide the dough into three pieces and roll each piece out separately to a thickness of 1/16 inch. Cut into rectangles or small rounds. While rolling dough lift it several times add flour underneath it on the board. Also keep the rolling pin well floured as you roll.

6. Place the crackers on a greased cookie tin and prick each with a fork.

7. Bake in a preheated 350 degree oven for 10 minutes. Then turn the crackers with a spatula and bake for an additional 5 minutes.

8. When done let cool on a wire rack and store in an airtight container to preserve crispness. If crackers become moist they may be crisped by returning to the oven for a very few minutes.

SOURDOUGH GRAHAM CRACKERS

½ cup Room Temperature Sourdough Starter
¾ cup honey
½ cup butter
1½ tsp salt
1 tsp baking soda
1 TBS ginger
2½ cups graham flour
Yield: about 60 graham crackers

1. Prepare the Room Temperature Sourdough Starter following the directions in Chapter 4. Be sure to replenish your original starter before proceeding with the recipe.

2. Assemble all ingredients and utensils. Let all ingredients come to room temperature.

3. Heat the ¾ cup honey and ½ cup butter. Set aside for 15 minutes to cool.

4. Add 1½ tsp salt, 1 tsp baking soda, and 1 TBS ginger to the honey and butter. Stir in the ½ cup of sourdough starter and 2½ cups of graham flour.

5. Knead lightly and place in a warm 85 degree spot for 45 minutes.

6. Roll out to a thickness of 1/8 inch and cut into 3 inch squares. This is a very tender dough and will tear easily if too much pressure is used on the rolling pin. Make sure the board is well covered with graham flour before beginning to roll and be sure to keep flour under the dough and the rolling pin well floured.

7. Place the squares on a greased cookie sheet. Prick all over with a fork to avoid puffing.

8. Bake in a 350 degree oven for 15-20 minutes.

9. Cool thoroughly before storing in an airtight container to insure crispness. If the crackers lose their crispness it may be restored by putting them on a cookie tin and placing it in an oven at 250 degrees for about 10 minutes.

SOURDOUGH RUSKS — SOURDOUGH ZWIEBACK

This recipe give you two baked goods for the effort of one. Sourdough Rusks are the product of the first baking and those which aren't eaten right away are returned to the oven to produce Sourdough Zwieback.

1 cup Room Temperature Sourdough Starter
½ cup butter
½ cup sugar
2 eggs
1 tsp baking soda
1 tsp vanilla
½ tsp salt
3-4 cups flour
Yield: about 20 sweet biscuits (Rusks) and/or Zwieback

1. Prepare the Room Temperature Sourdough Starter following the directions in Chapter 4. Be sure to replenish your original starter before proceeding with the recipe.

2. Assemble all ingredients and utensils. Let all ingredients come to room temperature.

3. Cream together ½ cup butter and ½ cup sugar.

4. Beat 2 eggs and stir them into the butter and sugar.

5. Stir in 1 cup of room temperature sourdough starter and 1 tsp baking soda, followed by 1 tsp vanilla and ½ tsp salt.

6. Stir in 3-4 cups of flour ½ cup at a time, stirring well after each addition until the dough leaves the sides of the pan.

7. Turn the dough onto a floured board and knead in enough additional flour to make a smooth satiny dough. Roll the dough out to a thickness of about ⅓ inch. Cut it with a large biscuit cutter or doughnut cutter (with the hole removed) into circles of about 2½ inches in diameter. Place these on a greased cookie sheet. Brush the tops with cooking oil.

8. Set the cookie sheet in a warm 85 degree spot for 45 minutes.

9. Bake in a preheated 400 degree oven for 15-20 minutes or until the tops are browned and done.

10. Serve hot those which you wish to eat as Rusks.

11. Split the remaining rusks and replace them on the cookie sheet and put it back in the oven at 250 degrees. Bake for 10 minutes then turn off the heat and leave the rusks in the oven until they are thoroughly dry and crisp. They are now Zwieback.

Chapter 7
Sourdough White Breads,
Rolls & Biscuits

This chapter leads you into the exciting world of breadmaking. You will find that the recipes in this chapter are totally independent of each other. This means that each recipe is wholly contained and thus you can bake each recipe from start to finish without having to read paragraphs from several different pages. Also you don't have to bake each recipe in sequential order to produce fine bread.

If you have never baked bread before, you will find that the no-knead recipes are good beginning recipes. As you become more familiar with the steps involved you can easily progress into the other breads. One of the author's favorites is the Sourdough White Bread 1 recipe which produces exceptional loaves of bread.

Now, with the information gathered in Chapters 1 thru 4 kept in mind, on with your sourdough adventure.

NO-KNEAD SOURDOUGH BREAD

> 1½ cups Primary Batter "B"
> ½ cup warm milk
> 1½ tsp salt
> 2 TBS sugar
> 2 TBS cooking oil or melted shortening
> 1 egg
> 2½ cups flour

Yield: 1 loaf.

1 . Prepare the Primary Batter "B" following the directions in Chapter 4. Be sure that you return one cup of the batter to your sourdough starter container before adding any other ingredients.

2. Assemble all ingredients and utensils. Let all ingredients come to room temperature.

3. In a warm 4-quart bowl mix the milk, salt, sugar and cooking oil together.

4. Beat the egg well and mix it thoroughly into the mixture in Step 3.

5. Add the 1½ cups of Primary Batter "B" and mix well again.

6. Add 2½ cups of the flour, ½ cup at a time, and beat vigorously until all the flour is blended in. Scrape down the sides of the bowl.

7. Cover the bowl and set it in a warm 85 degree place for about 2 hours for proofing. When the dough has doubled in bulk stir it down thoroughly.

8. Pour it into a well greased loaf pan and spread it out evenly. Pat the top smooth with floured hands.

9. Cover with a cloth and let rise in a warm 85 degree place until it reaches about 1 inch from the top of the pan. About 1 hour 45 minutes.

10. Bake in a preheated 375 degree oven for 45 minutes. When the bread starts to shrink away from the sides of the pan it is done.

11 . When done, remove the bread from the oven and brush the top with melted butter. Place on a wire rack to cool immediately.

SOURDOUGH WHITE BREAD I

This white bread forms the basis for many variations in flavor and texture which are suggested later. It produces an unexcelled sourdough white bread which many have claimed is the best bread that they have ever eaten.

> 3 cups Primary Batter "A"
> 6-6½ cups white flour
> 2 TBS sugar
> 2 tsp salt
> 1½ cups milk
> 2 TBS melted butter

Yield: 2 loaves.

1. Prepare the Primary Batter "A" following the directions in Chapter 4. Be sure that you have returned 1 cup of your batter to your sourdough starter container before adding other ingredients.

2. Assemble all ingredients and utensils. Let all ingredients come to room temperature.

3. Place the 3 cups of Primary Batter "A" in a warm, 4-quart or larger bowl. Stir in 1 cup of the flour and the 2 TBS sugar.

4. Add the salt, warm milk, and melted butter. If you are using unpasteurized milk, it is wise to scald it first and then let it cool to room temperature.

5. Stir in enough additional flour (approximately 4 cups) until the dough is too stiff to stir with a spoon.

6. Turn the dough onto a floured bread board or pastry cloth and knead in enough additional flour (about 1-1½ cups) to make the dough smooth and elastic.

7. Lightly grease the outside of the dough with shortening and place in a lightly greased bowl (4-quart or larger). Cover with a cloth and place in a warm, dry place at 85 degrees until the dough doubles in bulk. This will take about 2 hours. When the imprint of two fingers pressed about ½ inch into the dough remains, the dough is considered to be doubled in bulk.

8. When the dough has doubled, punch it down with a closed fist to release the leavening gases and return it to the same warm place for a second rising. Let rise again for 30 minutes.

9. After the second rising, turn the dough onto a floured board and divide it into two equal parts. Fold each part over itself and pinch the edges to seal the loaf. Place the loaves with the pinched edges down in well greased loaf pans. Each pan should be about half full. Brush the tops with melted butter and place the pans in a warm spot to rise again for about 1½ hours. This rising is done when two fingers pressed about ½ inch into the loaves causes the impression to remain.

10. In a preheated 375 degree oven place the pans on the center rack. Bake for approximately 45 minutes or until the bread shrinks away from the sides of the pans and is well browned on the tops.

11. Take the bread from the oven and remove from the pans at once. To prevent soggy bread, turn the loaves on their sides on a wire rack to cool. For a softer crust brush the tops of the loaves with melted butter.

SOURDOUGH WHITE BREAD II

3 cups Primary Batter "A"
2 TBS melted butter
¼ cup sugar
2 tsp salt
2½ cups flour
Yield: 2 loaves.

1. Prepare Primary Batter "A" following the directions in Chapter 4. Be sure to return 1 cup of the batter to your sourdough starter container before adding any other ingredients.

2. Assemble all ingredients and utensils. Let all ingredients come to room temperature.

3. Put the 3 cups of Primary Batter "A" in a warm 4-quart or larger bowl.

4. Add the 2 TBS melted butter, ¼ cup sugar and the 2 tsp salt, mixing well.

5. Add 2 cups of the flour, one-half cup at time, and mix well.

6. Turn onto a floured board and knead until smooth and satiny. This will take about ½ additional cup of flour.

7. Grease hands well and shape the dough into two loaves. Place the loaves in two well-greased loaf pans and put the pans in a warm dry place (85 degrees) for proofing. Let rise for about 2 hours or until doubled in bulk. Test for doubled in bulk by seeing if the imprint of two fingers pressed into the dough remains.

8. If it remains, then place the pans in a preheated 350 degree oven and bake for 1 hour or until it is golden brown. Remove from oven when the bread shrinks from the sides of the pans and produces a hollow sound when thumped.

9. Remove from pans and brush the tops with melted butter. Place on a wire rack to cool.

SOURDOUGH BANANA BREAD (NO-KNEAD)

This bread is ideal to serve with breakfast for those who don't feel like eating an extremely sweet bread so early in the morning. It is one of the author's favorites.

1½ cups Primary Batter "B"
1 cup sugar
1 tsp baking soda
1 tsp salt
⅓ cup shortening
1 egg
1 cup mashed bananas
1 cup flour

Yield: 1 loaf.

1. Prepare the Primary Batter "B" following the directions given in Chapter 4. Be sure that you have returned 1 cup of your batter to your sourdough starter container before adding any other ingredients.

2. Assemble all ingredients and utensils. Let all ingredients come to room temperature.

3. Put the 1½ cups of Primary Batter "B" in a warm bowl. Stir in the 1 cup of sugar, and the 1 tsp of baking soda and the 1 tsp of salt.

4. Melt the shortening and stir it into the batter.

5. Lightly beat the egg and stir it into the batter.

6. Stir in the 1 cup of mashed bananas and slowly stir in the 1 cup of flour until just moist.

7. Pour into a greased loaf pan.

8. Bake in a 350 degree oven for 1 hour or slightly longer (1 hr. 15 min.). The bread is done when a toothpick comes out clean.

9. Remove from oven when done and let cool thoroughly before serving. This bread tastes especially good when reheated just before serving.

SOURDOUGH COLONIAL BREAD (NO-KNEAD)

This no-knead sourdough bread will prove to be a great favorite with your family. The nuts and raisins provide the bread with a unique taste and texture.

> 1½ cups Primary Batter "B"
> ½ cup milk
> 1 TBS sugar
> 1 tsp salt
> 1½ tsp baking soda
> ½ cup chopped nuts
> ½ cup chopped raisins
> 1-1½ cups flour

Yield: 1 9-inch round loaf.

1. Prepare the Primary Batter "B" following the directions in Chapter 4. Be sure that you have returned 1 cup of the batter to your sourdough starter container before adding any other ingredients to it.

2. Assemble all ingredients and utensils. Let all ingredients come to room temperature.

3. Place the 1½ cups of Primary Batter "B" in a warm bowl. Stir in the ½ cup of milk.

4. Stir in the 1 TBS of sugar, the 1 tsp of salt and the 1½ tsp of baking soda. Stir in the ½ cup of chopped nuts and the ½ cup of chopped raisins.

5. Stir in the flour. You should have a soft dough. Put the dough in a 9-inch round pan. Cover with a cloth and put in a warm place at 85 degrees for 1 hour and 15 minutes.

6. Bake in a 300 degree oven for 1 hour or until a toothpick stuck in the middle of the loaf comes out clean.

7. When done, remove from oven and brush the top with melted butter.

SOURDOUGH SPIDER BREAD (NO-KNEAD)

This recipe is ideal for camp cooking. It also comes in very handy when a quick bread is needed and you don't have time to go through all the proofing periods that most breads call for. It is a hearty coarse bread which goes extremely well with bacon and eggs or with any type of game.

> 1½ cups Primary Batter "B"
> ⅓ cup bacon fat or butter
> 2 tsp baking soda
> 1 tsp salt
> 1 cups flour

Yield: 1 round loaf.

1. Prepare the Primary Batter "B" following the directions in Chapter 4. Be sure that you have returned 1 cup of the batter to your sourdough starter container before proceeding with the recipe.

2. Assemble all ingredients and utensils. Let all ingredients come to room temperature.

3. Mix the ⅓ cup of bacon fat, the 2 tsp of baking soda and the 1 tsp of salt into the Primary Batter "B".

4. Add the 1 cup of flour stirring continually. It will make a thick soft dough.

5. Turn the dough onto a floured board, turn it over and pick it up. It should now have the consistency that you can shape it into a round loaf the size of your frying pan. A steep sided frying pan works best for this recipe. If not thick enough, put it back on the floured board, turn it over and pick it up again. Repeat this until you can form the loaf.

6. Heat the pan over a moderately high flame and grease it liberally with bacon fat or butter. When hot, put the loaf into the pan and cook it over a moderately low flame.

7. Cook it 9-10 minutes on each side and serve hot. The finished loaf will be about 1 inch thick if you used a 9-10 inch frying pan.

Note: This bread remains soft and good when cool. Or it can be reheated by wrapping it in a piece of aluminum foil and placing it in an oven or a frying pan for a few minutes.

SOURDOUGH HERB BREAD I

This herb bread is just the thing to serve when you want to give your guests and family something different and zesty.

> 3 cups Primary Batter "A"
> 6-6½ cups white flour
> 2 TBS sugar
> 2 tsp salt
> 1½ cups milk
> 2 TBS melted butter
> 2 tsp thyme
> 1 tsp oregano
> 1 tsp basil
> ½ tsp sage

Yield. 2 loaves.

1. Prepare the Primary Batter "A" following the directions in Chapter 4. Be sure that you have returned 1 cup of your batter to your sourdough starter container before adding other ingredients.

2. Assemble all ingredients and utensils. Let all ingredients come to room temperature.

3. Place the 3 cups of Primary Batter "A" in a warm, 4-quart or larger bowl. Stir in 1 cup of the flour and the 2 TBS sugar.

4. Add the salt, warm milk, and melted butter. If you are using unpasteurized milk, it is wise to scald it first and then let it cool to room temperature. Crush the herbs very finely. A mortar and pestle works best for this. When finely crushed add them directly.

5. Stir in enough additional flour (approximately 4 cups) until the dough is too stiff to stir with a spoon.

6. Turn the dough onto a floured bread board or pastry cloth and knead in enough additional flour (about 1-1½ cups) to make the dough smooth and elastic.

7. Lightly grease the outside of the dough with shortening and place in a lightly greased bowl (4-quart or larger). Cover with a cloth and place in a warm, dry place at 85 degrees until the dough doubles in bulk. This will take about 2 hours. When the imprint of two fingers pressed about ½ inch into the dough remains, the dough is considered to be doubled in bulk.

8. When the dough has doubled, punch it down with a closed fist to release the leavening gases and return it to the same warm place for a second rising. Let rise again for 30 minutes.

9. After the second rising, turn the dough onto a floured board and divide it into two equal parts. Fold each part over itself and pinch the edges to seal the loaf. Place the loaves with the pinched edges down in well greased loaf pans. Each pan should be about half full. Brush the tops with melted butter and place the pans in a warm spot to rise again for about 1½ hours.

10. In a preheated 375 degree oven place the pans on the center rack. Bake for approximately 45 minutes or until the bread shrinks away from the sides of the pans and is well browned on the tops.

11. Take the bread from the oven and remove from the pans at once. To prevent soggy bread, turn the loaves on their sides on a wire rack to cool. For a softer crust, brush the tops of the loaves with melted butter.

SOURDOUGH HERB BREAD II

> 3 cups Primary Batter "A"
> 6-6½ cups white flour
> 2 TBS sugar
> 2 tsp salt
> 1½ cups milk
> ¼ cup shortening
> herb filling - recipe below

Yield: 2 loaves.

1. Prepare the Primary Batter "A" following the directions in Chapter 4. Be sure that you have returned 1 cup of your batter to your sourdough starter container before adding other ingredients.

2. Assemble all ingredients and utensils. Let all ingredients come to room temperature.

3. Place the 3 cups of Primary Batter "A" in a warm, 4-quart bowl. Stir in 1 cup of the flour and the 2 TBS sugar.

4. Add the salt, the 1½ cups of milk at room temperature, and the melted shortening.

5. Stir in enough additional flour (approximately 4 cups) until the dough is too stiff to stir with a spoon.

6. Turn the dough onto a floured board or pastry cloth and knead in enough additional flour (about 1-1½ cups) to make the dough smooth and elastic.

7. Lightly grease the outside of the dough with shortening and place in a lightly greased bowl. Cover with a cloth and place in a warm, dry place at 85 degrees until the dough doubles in bulk. This will take about 2 hours.

8. While the dough is doubling in bulk prepare the Herb Filling following the recipe below.

9. When the dough has doubled, punch it down with a closed fist, fold the dough over the impression left by your fist and turn it over. Cover it again and place in a warm place at 85 degrees for proofing for an additional 30 minutes.

10. After the second rising, turn the dough onto a floured board and divide it into two equal parts. With your hand, flatten out each piece of dough until it is about ¼ inch thick and about 9 inches wide.

11. Brush the top of the dough with a lightly beaten egg and then spread the Herb Filling over it to about 1inch from the edges. Roll the dough up and pinch the final edges to seal.

12. Place the loaves in greased loaf pans with the seam side down. Brush the tops with melted butter and then put the pans in a warm 85 degree place to proof for 1-1½ hours.

13. After the final proofing, place the pans in a preheated 375 degree oven near the center of the oven. Bake for approximately 45 minutes or until the bread begins to shrink away from the sides of the pan and the loaf emits a hollow sound when thumped.

14. When done, remove from the oven and turn out onto a wire rack to cool.

Herb Filling

2 cups finely chopped parsley
2 cups finely chopped onions
1 large clove garlic, minced
2 TBS butter
2 eggs
¾ tsp salt
pepper to taste

1 . Cook the parsley, onions and clove of garlic in the 2 TBS of butter over moderate heat, until they are wilted but not yet browned. Let cool.

2. Slightly beat the 2 eggs. Reserve 2 TBS of the eggs to use to brush the dough with in Step 11. Add the rest of the eggs to the onion, parsley, garlic mixture and stir. Add the salt and pepper and stir again.

SOURDOUGH DILL BREAD

3 cups Primary Batter "A"
6-6½ cups flour
2 TBS sugar
1 cup milk
1 cup small curd creamed cottage cheese
2 TBS melted butter
2 tsp salt
¼ tsp baking soda
2 TBS instant minced onion
3 tsp dill seed

Yield: 2 loaves.

1. Prepare the Primary Batter "A" following the directions in Chapter 4. Be sure to return one cup of your batter to your sourdough starter container before adding other ingredients.

2. Assemble all ingredients and utensils. Let all ingredients come to room temperature.

3. Put the 3 cups of Primary Batter "A" in a warm 4-quart bowl. Stir in 1 cup of the flour and the 2 TBS sugar. Stir until well blended. Set aside.

4. Add the cottage cheese to the 1 cup of milk and stir over low heat until lukewarm. Add the 2 TBS melted butter, the 2 tsp salt, the ¼ tsp baking soda, the 2 TBS of instant minced onion and the 3 tsp of dill seed. Stir well.

5. Add the milk mixture to the sourdough batter and stir well.

6. Add 4 more cups of flour, ½ cup at a time, mixing well after each addition.

7. Put 2 cups of flour on the bread board and turn the dough out onto it. Knead in enough flour (about 1-1½ cups) to make the dough smooth and satiny.

8. Form into a round ball and place in a well greased bowl. Cover the dough with a cloth and place it in a warm (85 degree) place for proofing. In about 2 hours the dough will have doubled in bulk. Test by seeing if the impression of two fingers remains.

9. When doubled in bulk, punch down and knead slightly in the bowl.

10. Divide the dough into two pieces and shape into two loaves. Put the loaves into two well greased loaf pans and cover. Place the pans in a warm (85 degree) place and let rise again for about 1½-1¾ hours.

11. Bake in a preheated 375 degree oven for 45 minutes. The bread is done when the loaves shrink away from the sides of the pans and a thumping produces a hollow sound.

12. When done, remove the pans from the oven and the loaves from the pans. Set them on a wire rack to cool.

Sourdough Caraway Bread

Substitute 3 TBS caraway seed for the dill seed and omit the onion entirely, in the above recipe. Follow all the directions as given.

SOURDOUGH CHEESE BREAD

This bread is one of the author's favorites as a base for creamed foods and also for toast.

    1½ cups Primary Batter "B"
    1 cup milk
    ¼ cup sugar
    2 tsp salt
    2 TBS melted butter
    1 egg
    1½ cups grated sharp cheddar cheese
    3½-4½ cups white flour
Yield: 2 loaves.

1. Prepare the Primary Batter "B" following the directions in Chapter 4. Be sure that you have returned 1 cup of the batter to your sourdough starter container before proceeding with the recipe.

2. Assemble all ingredients and utensils. Let all ingredients come to room temperature.

3. Put the 1½ cups of Primary Batter "B" in a warm bowl. Heat the milk to lukewarm and stir it into the batter. Stir in the ¼ cup of sugar and the 2 tsp of salt.

4. Beat the egg and stir it and the 2 TBS of melted butter into the batter.

5. Stir into the batter the 1½ cups of grated sharp cheddar cheese.

6. Stir in 3½ cups of flour ½ cup at a time, stirring after each addition. When the dough has begun to leave the sides of the bowl, turn it out onto a floured bread board and knead until it is smooth and satiny.

7. Shape into loaves and place in greased loaf pans. Brush the tops with melted butter and cover the pans. Set in a warm 85 degree spot for proofing for 2 hours or until doubled in bulk.

8. Bake in a preheated 375 degree oven for 30 minutes. This bread browns extremely easily. If it is getting too brown and the baking time is not nearly over, cover the bread with a tent of aluminum foil to retard the browning action.

9. When done, remove from the pans and place on wire racks to cool.

SOURDOUGH PEANUT BUTTER BREAD
(NO-KNEAD)

This easy to make bread is just great with jelly or jam and is nutritious at the same time.

> 1½ cups Primary Batter "B"
> ½ cup firmly packed brown sugar
> ½ cup milk
> ½ cup peanut butter
> ½ tsp salt
> 2 TBS butter
> ½ tsp baking soda
> 2½ cups white flour

Yield: 1 loaf

1. Prepare Primary Batter "B" following the directions in Chapter 4. Be sure that you have returned 1 cup of the batter to your sourdough starter storage container before adding other ingredients.

2. Assemble all ingredients and utensils. Let all ingredients come to room temperature.

3. Put the 1½ cups of Primary Batter "B" in a 2 quart or larger bowl. Stir in the ½ cup of brown sugar and ½ cup of milk.

4. Heat the peanut butter until it just melts. Let cool slightly and then stir it into the batter with ½ tsp salt, 2 TBS of melted butter, and ½ tsp baking soda.

5. Stir in the 2½ cups of flour and pour the batter into a 9x5 loaf pan. Set the pan in a warm 85 degree place for 30 minutes.

6. Bake in a preheated 350 degree oven for 45 minutes or until a toothpick inserted into the center comes out clean.

7. Remove from pan and set on wire rack to cool.

SOURDOUGH PROTEIN SESAME BREAD

This is an incredibly healthy bread. It contains about 10 percent of an adults daily protein requirement. This moist bread is the recipe of Evelyn Cleveland of Williamsville, New York.

      1½ cups Primary Batter "B"
      1 cup chicken stock (or 2 tsp granular chicken boullion
              dissolved in 1 cup hot water)
      1½ TBS cooking oil
      1½ TBS honey
      1½ cups whole wheat flour
      1 egg
      ½ tsp salt
      ½ cup sesame seeds
      ¼ cup soy flour
      2 cups white flour
Yield. 2 loaves

1. Prepare the Primary Batter "B" following the directions in Chapter 4. Be sure that you return 1 cup of the batter to your sourdough starter storage container before adding any ingredients.

2. Assemble all ingredients and utensils. Let all ingredients come to room temperature.

3. Put the 1 cup of stock, 1½ TBS cooking oil and 1½ TBS honey in a pan and heat until lukewarm. This means the temperature of the inside of your wrist.

4. Put the 1½ cups of Primary Batter "B" in a 2 quart or larger bowl and stir the stock mixture into it. Stir in 1½ cups of whole wheat flour.

5. Add the 1 egg, ½ tsp salt, ½ cup sesame seeds and ¼ cup of soy flour. Stir well.

6. Add 1 cup of white flour and stir well. Turn out onto a floured board and knead in the remaining 1 cup of white flour or until the dough is smooth and elastic.

7. Put the dough in a greased bowl, turn over, cover, and set in a warm 85 degree spot for 2 hours or until doubled in bulk.

8. When doubled form two loaves from the dough and put into 8x4 loaf pans. Brush with a mixture of egg and water and sprinkle with sesame seeds. Put the pans in a warm 85 degree spot and let rise again until double in bulk, about 1¾ hours.

9. Bake in a preheated 375 degree oven for 30-35 minutes or until the dough leaves the sides of the pan.

10. When done remove from pans and place on sides on wire racks to cool.

SOURDOUGH SWEET POTATO BREAD

1½ cups Primary Batter "B"
¼ cup unsulphured molasses
2 TBS bacon fat
1 tsp salt
1 tsp baking soda
1 cup mashed and strained cooked sweet potatoes
2½ cups white flour

Yield: 1 large loaf

1 . Prepare the Primary Batter "B" following the directions in Chapter 4. Be sure that you have returned 1cup of the batter to your sourdough storage container before proceeding with the recipe.

2. Assemble all ingredients and utensils. Let all ingredients come to room temperature.

3. Put the 1½ cups of Primary Batter "B" in a large warm bowl. Stir in ¼ cup of unsulphured molasses and 2 TBS bacon fat.

4. Stir in 1 tsp salt, 1 tsp baking soda and 1 cup of mashed and sieved cooked sweet potatoes. Stir until thoroughly mixed.

5. Stir in 2 cups of white flour, ½ cup at a time, stirring well after each addition.

6. Turn the dough out onto a floured board and knead in enough additional flour, about ½ cup, to make the dough smooth and satiny.

7. Place the dough in a greased bowl, turn the dough over, cover the bowl, and place it in a warm 85 degree spot until it has doubled in bulk. This will take slightly over 2 hours.

8. After the dough has doubled in bulk turn it onto a floured board and knead it lightly for 10-15 strokes. Then form it into one large round loaf and place it on a cookie tin which has been greased and sprinkled with cornmeal.

9. Place the sheet in a warm 85 degree spot and cover the dough with a cloth suspended between two inverted water tumblers to prevent the cloth from resting on the dough.

10. When the dough has doubled in bulk again (about 1¾ hours) place the pan in a preheated 400 degree oven and bake for 45 minutes or until the dough sounds hollow when thumped on the bottom. Cool on a wire rack.

SOURDOUGH SQUASH BREAD

1½ cups Primary Batter "B"
½ cup milk
2 TBS sugar
1 tsp salt
1 cup cooked mashed squash
3¼-4¼ cups white flour
Yield. 2 loaves

1. Prepare Primary Batter "B" following the directions in Chapter 4. Be sure that you have returned 1 cup of the batter to your sourdough starter container before continuing with the recipe.

2. Assemble all ingredients and utensils. Let all ingredients come to room temperature.

3. Put the 1½ cups of Primary Batter "B" in 4-quart bowl. Add the ½ cup milk, the 2 TBS of sugar, 1 tsp salt, and 1 cup of cooked mashed squash. Stir well.

4. Add 2 cups of white flour, ½ cup at a time stirring well.

5. When the dough begins to leave the sides of the bowl, but is still sticky, turn it out onto a heavily floured (1½ cups) bread board and knead until smooth and satiny (this will use about ¾ cups more). Place in a greased bowl, turn over and set in a warm 85 degree place for proofing.

6. When the dough has doubled in bulk (about 2 hours) punch it down and let rise again until double in bulk. This will take 30 to 45 minutes.

7. Turn the dough onto a floured bread board and divide the dough into two pieces. Form two loaves and put in greased loaf pans.

8. Set the pans in a warm 85 degree place to rise until double in bulk again. This will take about 2 hours.

9. Brush tops with butter and bake in a preheated 375 degree oven for 45 minutes or until the bread begins to leave the sides of the pans.

10. When done remove from pans and place loaves on their side to cool.

SOURDOUGH SAUSAGE BREAD

The recipe produces a bread which is a whole meal in itself. The sausage gives the bread a filling and tangy substance.

> 1½ cups Primary Batter "B"
> 2 TBS sugar
> 1 tsp salt
> ½ tsp baking soda
> 1 cup tomato juice
> 3 to 3½ cups white flour
> 1 lb cooked and well drained sausage

Yield: 2 long loaves or 1 large round loaf

1. Prepare the Primary Batter "B" following the directions in Chapter 4. Be sure that you have returned 1 cup of the batter to the starter before adding any ingredients.

2. Assemble all ingredients and utensils. Let all ingredients come to room temperature.

3. Put the 1½ cups of Primary Batter "B" in a 2 quart or larger bowl. Add the 2 TBS sugar, 1 tsp salt, ½ tsp baking soda and 1 cup tomato juice. Stir well.

4. Stir in 1 pound of cooked and finely crumbled sausage after it has had a chance to drain well and to cool.

5. Add 3 cups of white flour ½ cup at a time stirring until the dough begins to leave the sides of the bowl.

6. Turn out onto a floured bread board and knead in enough additional flour (about ½ cup) to make the dough smooth and satiny. Do not over knead. Place the dough in a greased bowl, turn it over, cover the bowl and set it in a warm 85 degree spot until it doubles in bulk, about 2-2½ hours.

7. When the dough has doubled in bulk, turn it out onto a floured board and form two loaves by the following method. Divide the dough into two pieces. Gently knead each piece about 8 to 10 times then set aside for 15 minutes to rest.

8. Flatten each piece out with your hand into a large oval bowl and with the heel of your hand make an indentation the length of the oval. Fold the back half of the oval towards yourself. Pinch the edges to seal the dough and then repeat the operation again. Gently round the loaf with your hands and place it on a cookie tin which has been greased and sprinkled with cornmeal. Do the same with the other piece of dough. Place the tray in a warm 85 degree place until the loaves double in bulk. This will take about 1½ hours.

9. Bake in a preheated 400 degree oven for 40 to 45 minutes or until the loaves sound hollow when thumped on the bottom.

10. Cool on wire racks.

SOURDOUGH CRANBERRY BREAD (NO-KNEAD)

        1½ cups Primary Batter "B"
        2 oranges
        ½ tsp salt
        ½ tsp baking soda
        2 eggs well beaten
        4 TBS butter melted
        1⅓ cups sugar
        3 cups flour
        2 cups chopped cranberries
        1 cup chopped nuts
Yield. 1 9x9x4 sweet bread

1. Prepare Primary Batter "B" following the directions in Chapter 4. Be sure that you have returned 1 cup of the batter to your sourdough starter container before continuing with the recipe.

2. Assemble all ingredients and utensils. Let all ingredients come to room temperature.

3. Put the 1½ cups of Primary Batter "B" in 2-quart or larger bowl.

4. Cut the oranges in half, squeeze out the juice and strain. Add ⅓ cup to the batter.

5. Grate the rind and add it to the batter and stir.

6. Add the ½ tsp salt, ½ tsp soda and the 2 beaten eggs. Stir well.

7. Add the 4 TBS of melted butter, 1⅓ cups of sugar and 3 cups of flour (1 cup at a time) stirring until well mixed.

8. Fold in the 2 cups of chopped cranberries and 1 cup of chopped nuts.

9. Spoon the batter into a greased and floured 9x9x4 loaf pan.

10. Bake at 375 degrees for 1 hour to 1 hour and 15 minutes, or until a straw or toothpick comes out clean when stuck into the bread.

11. Remove from pan and cool on wire rack. Drizzle powdered sugar icing over the loaf for a festive sight.

SOURDOUGH YOGURT ORANGE BREAD

This bread is a wonderful breakfast bread, especially when toasted. The recipe comes from Evelyn Cleveland of Williamsville, New York, who serves it to family and friends frequently.

1½ cups Primary Batter "B"
½ cup yogurt
1 egg
1½ TBS oil
¼ cup honey
½ cup orange juice
1 TBS grated orange rind
1 cup whole wheat flour
½ cup soy flour
1½ TBS sesame seeds
½ tsp salt
2 cups white flour

Yield: 2 loaves

1. Prepare the Primary Batter "B" following the directions in Chapter 4. Be sure that you have returned 1 cup of the batter to your sourdough starter before adding any other ingredients to it.

2. Assemble all ingredients and utensils. Let all ingredients come to room temperature.

3. Place the ½ cup of yogurt, 1 egg, 1½ TBS oil, ¼ cup honey, ½ cup orange juice, and 1 TBS grated orange rind in a pan and warm to lukewarm (the temperature of the inside of your wrist).

4. Add about half of this mixture to the 1½ cups of Primary Batter "B" in a 2 quart or larger bowl.

5. Add 2 cups of whole wheat flour stir well and then pour in the remainder of the warmed mixture. Add the ½ cup of soy flour, 1½ TBS of sesame seeds and ½ tsp salt. Stir well.

6. Add 1 cup of white flour, ½ cup at a time, stirring until the dough is too stiff to stir.

7. Turn the dough out onto a floured bread board and knead in the remaining 1 cup of white flour. Place in a greased bowl, turn over and cover. Set the bowl in a warm 85 degree place until doubled in bulk, about 2 hours.

8. When doubled form the dough into 2 loaves and place in greased 8x4 loaf pans. Brush the tops with orange juice and sprinkle the tops with sesame seeds.

9. Place the pans in a warm 85 degree spot to let the dough proof for an additional 1 hour 45 minutes.

10. Bake in a preheated 375 degree oven for 30-35 minutes or until the loaf leaves the sides of the pans.

SOURDOUGH DINNER ROLLS

1½ cups Primary Batter "B"
1 TBS sugar
½ tsp salt
2 TBS butter — melted
1 egg
1¾ cups flour
Yield: 10-20 good soft rolls depending on size.

1. Prepare the Primary Batter "B" following the directions in Chapter 4. Be sure that you have returned 1 cup of the batter to your sourdough starter container before continuing with the recipe.

2. Assemble all ingredients and utensils. Let all ingredients come to room temperature.

3. Put the 1½ cups of Primary Batter "B" in a warm bowl. Stir in the 1 TBS of sugar, the ½ tsp of salt, and 2 TBS of melted butter.

4. Beat the egg and stir it into the batter.

5. Add one cup of flour and beat until smooth. Turn this very soft dough onto a floured board and knead in enough additional flour to make the dough smooth and elastic. About ¾ cup.

6. Put the dough in a warm bowl and cover it. Set the bowl in a warm 85 degree spot for 2 hours or until it has doubled in bulk.

7. When doubled in a bulk, punch down the dough and recover it. Set it again in a warm place at 85 degrees until it has doubled in bulk again. This will take about 1⅓ hours.

8. Turn the dough out onto a floured board and roll the dough out to a thickness of ½ to ¾ inch. Pull the dough into pieces about the size of a lemon. Keeping hands well floured, shape these pieces into rolls and place them on a well greased cookie sheet.

9. Place the cookie sheet in a warm 85 degree place until they have doubled in bulk again. This will take about 30 minutes.

10. Bake in a preheated 400 degree oven for 20 minutes or until browned.

ROLL VARIATIONS

Using the Sourdough Dinner Rolls recipe, you can bake all sorts of rolls with little extra effort.

Sourdough Hamburger Roles

After rolling the dough to a thickness of ½ inch, use a three-inch cutter to cut out the rolls. Place at least 1 inch apart on the cookie sheet. Bake as directed.

Sourdough Parker House Rolls

After rolling the dough out to a thickness of ½ inch, cut with a 2-inch cutter. Using a knife, make a crease slightly off center across each roll. Turn the rolls over, brush them with melted butter and fold the larger part over the smaller. Bake as directed.

Sourdough Seed Rolls

When ready to be baked, rolls of any shape may be brushed with melted butter and sprinkled with poppy seed, celery seed, sesame seed, fennel seed, dill seed, or cumin seed, or any combination of these which pleases you.

SOURDOUGH BISCUITS

This recipe makes hearty, crusty biscuits which evoke the flavor of the old west.

> 1½ cups Primary Batter "B"
> 1 cup flour
> ½ tsp salt
> 1 TBS sugar
> ¼ tsp baking soda
> ¼ cup melted butter

Yield: 16 biscuits.

1. Prepare the Primary Batter "B" following the directions in Chapter 4. Be sure that you have returned 1 cup of the batter to your sourdough starter container before adding any other ingredients.

2. Assemble all ingredients and utensils. Let all ingredients come to room temperature.

3. Put the 1½ cups of Primary Batter "B" in a warm bowl.

4. Mix the 1 cup of flour, the ½ tsp salt, the 1 TBS sugar, and the ¼ tsp baking soda together and then sift the mixture into the batter while stirring gently. Just stir enough to wet the flour.

5. Turn onto a floured bread board or pastry cloth and knead for approximately ½ minute until you have a soft, just barely sticky dough.

6. Roll out with a floured rolling pin or pat out with your hands until the dough is approximately ¼ to ½ inch in thickness.

7. Using a biscuit cutter, cut out the biscuits, being careful not to turn the cutter while cutting.

8. Carefully lift out the biscuits and dip them in the melted butter. Place them close together on a 9-inch square pan and put the pan in a warm place for proofing for 30 minutes.

9. When the proofing period is over, place the pan in a preheated 375 degree oven. Let the biscuits bake for 30-35 minutes. Serve them hot as the texture hardens when the biscuits are cool. To reheat, place in a moistened paper bag, close the bag and then put it in the oven for 10 minutes at 350 degrees.

HELEN'S SOURDOUGH BISCUITS

1½ cups Primary Batter "B"
½ cup milk
2 cups flour
¾ tsp salt
1 TBS sugar
¼ tsp baking soda
Yield: about 14 biscuits.

1. Prepare the Primary Batter "B" following the directions in Chapter 4. Be sure that you have returned 1 cup of the batter to your sourdough starter container before adding other ingredients.

2. Assemble all ingredients and utensils. Let all ingredients come to room temperature.

3. Put the 1½ cups of Primary Batter "B" in a warm bowl. Stir in the ½ cup of milk and 1 cup of flour.

4. Combine separately the ¾ tsp salt, the 1 TBS sugar and the ¼ tsp baking soda. Fold gently into the batter.

5. Turn the dough out onto a generously floured board (about 1 cup of flour) and gently and softly knead in enough flour so that the dough can be patted out with the hands until it is about ½ inch thick.

6. Cut with a biscuit cutter being careful not to twist the cutter.

7. Gently lift out the biscuits and place in a 9-inch round or square cake pan. Crowd the biscuits slightly. Pat the tops with your fingers which have been dipped in melted butter.

8. Cover and place in a warm 85 degree place for proofing for 30 minutes.

9. Bake in a preheated 375 degree oven for 30 minutes and serve hot.

SOURDOUGH BUTTERMILK BISCUITS

1½ cups Primary Batter "B"
2 cups flour
1 tsp salt
½ tsp baking soda
½ cup butter
½ cup buttermilk
Yield: about 20 biscuits.

1 . Prepare the Primary Batter "B" following the directions in Chapter 4. Be sure that you have returned 1 cup of the batter to your sourdough starter container before proceeding with the recipe.

2. Assemble all ingredients and utensils. Let all ingredients come to room temperature.

3. Put the 2 cups of flour in a warm bowl. Add the 1 tsp of salt and the ½ tsp of baking soda. Using a fork or pastry blender cut the butter into the flour.

4. When the particles are about the size of cornmeal stir in the Primary Batter "B" and the ½ cup of buttermilk and stir until thoroughly moistened. The dough will be very soft.

5. Turn the dough out onto a lightly floured breadboard and knead for ½ minute.

6. Roll or pat the dough out until it is between ¼ and ½ inch thick.

7. Use a biscuit cutter to cut out the biscuits, being careful not to twist while cutting.

8. Lift the biscuits carefully and place on an ungreased cookie sheet, in a warm place for 30 minutes for proofing.

9. Put the cookie sheet in a preheated 450 degree oven for 15 minutes or until browned and done.

10. Serve immediately with butter.

Note: For high flaky biscuits, roll the dough out to ½ inch thick, while for low crusty biscuits roll it out until it is ⅓ inch thick. The sides are crusty if placed at least 1 inch apart on the cookie sheet, but will be soft and moist if the biscuits are placed close together.

SOURDOUGH CURRY CHEESE BISCUITS

1 cup Room Temperature Sourdough Starter
¼ tsp mustard powder
1 tsp baking soda
¾ tsp curry powder
½ tsp salt
½ cup grated cheddar cheese
¾ cup white flour
Yield: About 8 to 10 biscuits.

1. Prepare the Room Temperature Sourdough Starter following the directions in Chapter 4. Be sure to replenish your original starter before proceeding with the recipe.

2. Assemble all ingredients and utensils. Let all ingredients come to room temperature.

3. To the 1 cup of sourdough starter add the ¼ tsp mustard, the 1 tsp baking soda, and ¾ tsp curry powder.

4. Stir in the ½ tsp salt, the ½ cup of grated cheddar cheese and the ¾ cup of flour a small amount at a time. Stir only until the batter holds together.

5. Pat out to a thickness of about ½ inch and cut into 2 inch rounds with a cutter for doughnuts (minus the hole) or a cookie cutter.

6. Place on a greased cookie sheet and let rest for 30 minutes.

7. Bake at 400 degree F for 10 minutes or until golden brown.

SOURDOUGH MUFFINS

    1½ cups Primary Batter "B"
    1½ cups flour
    2 TBS sugar
    1 tsp salt
    ¼ cup shortening
    1 egg
Yield: about 12 muffins.

1. Prepare the Primary Batter "B" following the directions in Chapter 4. Be sure that you have returned 1 cup of the batter to your sourdough starter container before adding other ingredients.

2. Assemble all ingredients and utensils. Let all ingredients come to room temperature.

3. Put the 1½ cups of flour in a warm bowl. Add the 2 TBS of sugar and the 1 tsp of salt.

4. Use a pastry blender or a fork to cut in the shortening. When the mixture is the size of tiny peas make a hollow in the center.

5. Pour in the 1½ cups of Primary Batter "B" and slightly beaten egg. Stir only until the dry ingredients are just moist. The batter will be lumpy.

6. Fill greased muffin pan cups about ⅔ full.

7. Place in a warm place for 30 minutes for proofing.

8. Place the muffin pan in a preheated 400 degree oven for 25 minutes for baking.

9. Serve hot.

Note: Blueberry muffins can be made by quickly stirring 1 cup of fresh blueberries or 1 cup of well drained canned blueberries into the batter just before pouring into the muffin cups. Other fruits can also be added in place of blueberries.

SOURDOUGH APRICOT BRAN MUFFINS

These rich sweet muffins make a good dining companion to a curry dish or an entree prepared with a strong barbecue sauce.

> 1 cup Room Temperature Sourdough Starter
> ½ cup chopped dried apricots
> ½ cup apricot nectar
> 1 cup white flour
> ½ tsp baking soda
> 1 tsp salt
> ¼ cup shortening
> ½ cup bran flakes
> 1 egg
> ⅓ cup sugar (optional)

Yield: About 16 muffins

1 . Prepare the Room Temperature Sourdough Starter following the directions in Chapter 4. Be sure to replenish your original starter before proceeding with the recipe.

2. Assemble all ingredients and utensils. Let all ingredients come to room temperature.

3. Chop the ½ cup of dried apricots fine and pour the ½ cup of apricot nectar over them. Let rest for 45 minutes.

4. Place the 1 cup white flour, ½ tsp baking soda and 1 tsp salt in bowl. Use pastry blender or fork to cut the shortening into the flour mixture until the mixture is the size of small peas.

5. Add ½ cup of bran flakes, stir, and made a hole in the center.

6. Pour the 1 cup of room temperature starter in the hole.

7. Slightly beat the 1 egg and put it along with the ½ cup of apricot nectar and the ½ cup of chopped dried apricots in the mixture. For sweeter muffins add ⅓ cup of sugar at this time.

8. Stir only until the dry ingredients are just moist. The batter will be lumpy.

9. Fill greased muffin cups about ⅔ full. Place in a warm 85 degree spot for 30 minutes for proofing.

10. Bake in a preheated 400 degree oven for 25 minutes.

11 . Serve hot.

SOURDOUGH DUMPLINGS

1½ cups Primary Batter "B"
¼ cup shortening
1 cup flour
1 tsp salt
1½ tsp baking soda
¼ cup heavy cream or evaporated milk
Yield: about 14 dumplings.

1 . Prepare the Primary Batter "B" following the directions in Chapter 4. Be sure that you have returned 1 cup of the batter to your sourdough starter container before adding other ingredients.

2. Assemble all ingredients and utensils. Let all ingredients come to room temperature.

3. Sift the 1 cup of flour, 1 tsp of salt and 1½ tsp of baking soda into a bowl. Using a pastry blender or a fork cut the ¼ cup of shortening into flour until the mixture resembles coarse cornmeal.

4. Stir in the 1½ cups of Primary Batter "B" gently, followed by the ¼ cup evaporated milk. Just moisten the flour-shortening mixture to make a soft dough. Stir as little as possible.

5. Drop tablespoonfuls of the dough gently onto the top of the stew that the dumplings will be a topping for. If possible, let them rest on the tops of pieces of chicken or vegetables, etc. , so that they will stay afloat until they have had a chance to rise.

6. Cover the top immediately and do not open until the 15 minute cooking time has expired. At this time, if a toothpick stuck in the dumplings comes out clean they are done.

Note: For added variety, try adding chopped parsley, chives, sage or thyme to your dumplings in small amounts. Select an herb which compliments the flavor of the main course.

SOURDOUGH POPOVERS

1 cup Room Temperature Sourdough Starter
1 tsp salt
2 TBS sugar
1 cup milk
1 cup white flour
4 eggs
Yield: 12 popovers

1. Prepare the Room Temperature Sourdough Starter following the directions in Chapter 4. Be sure to replenish your original starter before proceeding with the recipe.

2. Assemble all ingredients and utensils.   Let all ingredients come to room temperature.

3. Prepare your popover pans, teflon coated muffin tins, or glass custard cups. Grease them and place in a preheated 450 degree oven.

4. Place the 1 cup of sourdough starter in a 1-quart or larger bowl. Add 1 tsp salt, 2 TBS melted butter, 1 cup milk and 1 cup white flour. Stir to make a smooth batter.

5. Beat 4 eggs until light. Stir them into the batter and beat 6 to 7 minutes with an electric mixer or 10 minutes by hand.

6. Remove the popover pans or custard cups from the oven and pour the batter into them until they are ⅔ full.

7. Place them back in the 450 degree oven for 45 minutes. Then turn the oven off and let the popovers remain in the oven for 5 minutes.

8. Serve hot.

Note: If the popovers are not done they will fall when removed from the oven. You can test for doneness by removing one from the oven and observing if it falls.

Chapter 8
Sourdough Whole Grain Bread

Many of the great breads of the world use whole grain flours rather than white flour. Many more use a whole grain flour in conjunction with white flour. This chapter contains new recipes apart from the white bread recipes and produces great tasting and nourishing breads.

Whole grain flours are those which have not had part of the nutrients milled out of the grain for purposes of long storage, easy digestibility or decorative facade. With all of the vitamins, minerals, proteins and fatty acids present you get a much more healthy bread than when using only white flour. These factors also produce an added benefit. They give bread a wide variety of delicious tastes and textures. There is no reason to be satisfied with only white bread when you can expand your horizons by baking and eating fine quality sourdough whole wheat, rye, oatmeal, and graham breads. All these and many more are included in this chapter.

SOURDOUGH WHOLE WHEAT BREAD I

3 cups Primary Batter "A"
3-3½ cups white flour
¼ cup sugar
¼ cup melted shortening
1½ cups milk
3 tsp salt
3 cups whole wheat flour
Yield: 2 large loaves.

1. Prepare the Primary Batter "A" following the directions in Chapter 4. Be sure that you have returned 1 cup of the batter to your sourdough starter container before proceeding with the recipe.

2. Assemble all ingredients and utensils. Let all ingredients come to room temperature.

3. Place the 3 cups of Primary Batter "A" in a large warm bowl. Mix in 1 cup of the white flour and the ¼ cup of sugar.

4. Melt the shortening and add the 1½ cups of milk and the 3 tsp of salt to it. Heat until lukewarm and add to the batter. Mix well.

5. Add the 3 cups of whole wheat flour, ½ cup at a time, stirring well after each addition.

6. Add 1 more cup of white flour and stir well.

7. Turn onto a well floured board and knead in enough additional flour (about 1 - 1½ cups) to make the dough smooth and elastic.

8. Place the dough in a well greased bowl, turn over, cover and place in a warm 85 degree place for proofing. When the dough is doubled in bulk, which takes about 2 hours, punch down the dough and return it to the same warm place for an additional proofing of 30 minutes.

9. Divide the dough into two equal parts and form into loaves. Be sure that before forming into loaves you have kneaded for about 30 seconds to force out any large pockets of gas.

10. Place in well greased loaf pans with the dough just touching the ends of the pans. Cover and place in a warm 85 degree spot for proofing for about 1½ hours.

11. Bake in a preheated 375 degree oven for 45 minutes. When golden brown and the loaves have shrunk away from the sides of the pans they are done.

12. Remove from pans and place on wire racks to cool. Brush the tops with butter as soon as the loaves are placed on the racks.

SOURDOUGH WHOLE WHEAT BREAD II

If you have a whole wheat starter and would like a very strong hearty bread, this recipe is just the thing. It uses no white flour and because of this you will have loaves which are not quite as light as if you were using white flour.

> 3 cups Primary Batter "A" (made with whole wheat flour)
> 6-6½ cups whole wheat flour
> 2 TBS sugar
> 2 tsp salt
> 1½ cups milk
> 2 TBS melted butter

Yield: 2 loaves.

1. Prepare the Primary Batter "A" following the directions in Chapter 4, substituting whole wheat for white flour. Be sure that you have returned 1 cup of your batter to your whole wheat sourdough starter container before adding other ingredients.

2. Assemble all ingredients and utensils. Let all ingredients come to room temperature.

3. Place the 3 cups of Primary Batter "A" in a warm 4-quart or larger bowl. Stir in 1 cup of the flour and the 2 TBS sugar.

4. Add the salt, warm milk, and melted butter. If you are using unpasteurized milk it is wise to scald it first and then let it cool to room temperature.

5. Stir in enough additional flour (approximately 4 cups) until the dough is too stiff to stir with a spoon.

6. Turn the dough onto a floured bread board or pastry cloth and knead in enough additional flour (about 1-1½ cups) to make the dough smooth and elastic.

7. Lightly grease the outside of the dough with shortening and place in a lightly greased bowl (4-quart or larger). Cover with a cloth and place in a warm, dry place at 85 degrees until the dough doubles in bulk. This will take about 2 hours. When the imprint of two fingers pressed about ½ inch into the dough remains, the dough is considered to be doubled in bulk.

8. When the dough has doubled, punch it down with a closed fist to release the leavening gases and return it to the same warm place for a second rising. Let rise again for 30 minutes.

9. After the second rising, turn the dough onto a floured board and divide it into two equal parts. Fold each part over itself and pinch the edges to seal the loaf. Place the loaves with the pinched edges down in well greased loaf pans. Each pan should be about half full. Brush the tops with melted butter and place the pans in a warm spot to rise again for about 1½ hours. This rising is done when two fingers pressed about ½ inch into the loaves causes the impression to remain.

10. In preheated 375 degree oven place the pans on the center rack. Bake for approximately 45 minutes or until the bread shrinks away from the sides of the pans and is well browned on the tops.

11. Take the bread from the oven and remove from the pans at once. To prevent soggy bread turn the loaves on their sides on a wire rack to cool. For a softer crust brush the tops of the loaves with melted butter.

Note: To give the bread an additional flavor, add ¼ cup of wheat germ and ¼ cup of orange juice to the recipe in Step 4 and replace the sugar with molasses. Further additions which can enhance the texture and flavor of the bread are raisins, dates, figs, nuts of any kind, prunes or other such goodies when added in any combination up to ½ cup per recipe.

SOURDOUGH WHOLE WHEAT ROLLS I

1½ cups Primary Batter "B"
1 TBS sugar
1/2 tsp salt
2 TBS butter - melted
1 egg
1¾ cups whole wheat flour.
Yield: 10-20 good soft rolls, depending on size.

1. Prepare the Primary Batter "B" following the directions in Chapter 4. Be sure that you have returned 1 cup of the batter to your sourdough starter container before continuing with the recipe.

2. Assemble all ingredients and utensils. Let all ingredients come to room temperature.

3. Put the 1½ cups of Primary Batter "B" in a warm bowl. Stir in the 1 TBS of sugar, the ½ tsp of salt and 2 TBS of melted butter.

4. Beat the egg and stir it into the batter.

5. Add one cup of whole wheat flour and beat until smooth. Turn this very soft dough onto a floured board and knead in enough additional whole wheat flour to make the dough smooth and elastic. About ¾ cup.

6. Put the dough in a warm bowl and cover it. Set the bowl in a warm 85 degree spot for 2 hours or until it has doubled in bulk.

7. When doubled in bulk punch down the dough and recover it. Set it again in a warm place at 85 degrees until it has doubled in bulk again. This will take about 1⅓ hours.

8. Turn the dough out onto a floured board and roll the dough out to a thickness of ½ to ¾ inch. Pull the dough into pieces about the size of a lemon. Keeping hands well floured, shape these pieces into rolls and place them on a well greased cookie sheet.

9. Place the cookie sheet in a warm 85 degree place until they have doubled in bulk again. This will take about 30 minutes.

10. Bake in a preheated 400 degree oven for 20 minutes or until browned.

SOURDOUGH WHOLE WHEAT ROLLS II

For a whole wheat roll which is totally whole wheat flour, use your whole wheat sourdough starter and make up the Primary Batter using whole wheat flour.

> 1½ cups Primary Batter "B"
> 1 TBS sugar
> ½ tsp salt
> 2 TBS butter - melted
> 1 egg
> 1¾ cups whole wheat flour

Yield: 10-20 good soft rolls, depending on size.

1. Prepare the Primary Batter "B" following the directions in Chapter 4. Be sure that you have returned 1 cup of the batter to your whole wheat sourdough starter container before continuing with the recipe.

2. Assemble all ingredients and utensils. Let all ingredients come to room temperature.

3. Put the 1½ cups of Primary Batter "B" in a warm bowl. Stir in the 1 TBS of sugar, the ½ tsp of salt, and 2 TBS of melted butter.

4. Beat the egg and stir it into the batter.

5. Add one cup of whole wheat flour and beat until smooth. Turn this very soft dough onto a floured board and knead in enough additional whole wheat flour to make the dough smooth and elastic. About ¾ cup.

6. Put the dough in a warm bowl and cover it. Set the bowl in a warm 85 degree spot for 2 hours or until it has doubled in bulk.

7. When doubled in bulk punch down the dough and recover it. Set it again in a warm place at 85 degrees until it has doubled in bulk again. This will take about 1⅓ hours.

8. Turn the dough out onto a floured board and roll the dough out to a thickness of ½ or ¾ inch. . Pull the dough into pieces about the size of a lemon. Keeping hands well floured, shape these pieces into rolls and place them on a well greased cookie sheet.

9. Place the cookie sheet in a warm 85 degree place until they have doubled in bulk again. This will take about 30 minutes.

10. Bake in a preheated 400 degree oven for 20 minutes or until browned.

SOURDOUGH WHOLE WHEAT MUFFINS

1½ cups Primary Batter "B"
1½ cups whole wheat flour
2 TBS brown sugar
1 tsp salt
¼ cup shortening
1 egg
Yield: about 12 muffins.

1. Prepare the Primary Batter "B" following the directions in Chapter 4. Be sure that you have returned 1 cup of the batter to your sourdough starter container before adding other ingredients.

2. Assemble all ingredients and utensils. Let all ingredients come to room temperature.

3. Put the 1½ cups of whole wheat flour in a warm bowl. Add the 2 TBS of brown sugar and the 1 tsp of salt.

4. Use a pastry blender or a fork to cut in the shortening. When the mixture is the size of tiny peas, make a hollow in the center.

5. Pour in the 1½ cups of Primary Batter "B" and slightly beaten egg. Stir only until the dry ingredients are just moist. The batter will be lumpy.

6. Fill greased muffin pan cups about ⅔ full.

7. Place in a warm place for 30 minutes for proofing.

8. Place the muffin pan in a preheated 400 degree oven for 25 minutes for baking.

9. Serve hot.

Note: Blueberry muffins can be made by quickly stirring 1 cup of fresh blueberries or 1 cup of well drained canned blueberries into the batter just before pouring into the muffin cups. Other fruits can also be added in placed of blueberries.

SOURDOUGH PRUNE WHOLE WHEAT BREAD

A beautiful dark loaf.

    1½ cups Primary Batter "B"
    2 TBS sugar
    1 tsp salt
    ½ tsp baking soda
    1 cup cooked prunes drained, pitted, and cut into quarters
    ¼ cup of the juice the prunes were cooked in
    2 cups whole wheat flour
    ¾-1 cup white flour
Yield: 1 loaf

1. Prepare the Primary Batter "B" following the directions in Chapter 4. Be sure that you have returned 1 cup of the batter to your sourdough starter before adding any ingredients.

2. Assemble all ingredients and utensils. Let all ingredients come to room temperature.

3. Put the 1½ cups of Primary Batter "B" in a 2-quart or larger warm bowl. Stir in 2 TBS sugar, 1 tsp salt, and ½ tsp baking soda.

4. Stir in 1 cup of pitted and quartered cooked prunes and ¼ cup of the juice in which the prunes were cooked.

5. Stir in 2 cups of whole wheat flour, ½ cup at a time, stirring well after each addition.

6. Stir in ½ cup of white flour, a little at a time, stirring well after each addition.

7. Turn the dough out onto a floured board and knead in enough additional flour, about ½ cup, to make the dough smooth and satiny.

8. Place the dough in a greased bowl, turn it over, cover the bowl and set it in a warm 85 degree spot for proofing until the dough doubles in bulk. This will take about 2 to 2½ hours.

9. After the dough has doubled in bulk, turn it out onto a floured board. Form into a loaf and place in a greased loaf pan. Cover the pan and place it in a 85 degree spot until doubled again in bulk. This will take about 1½ hours.

10. Bake in a preheated 375 degree oven for 45 minutes or until the dough leaves the sides of the pan.

11. When done remove from pan and place the loaf on its side to cool.

SOURDOUGH RYE BREAD

3 cups Primary Batter "A"
2 cups warm water
5 cups rye flour
3½ cups white flour
1 TBS caraway seed
2 tsp salt

Yield: 2 old-world type rye loaves.

1. Prepare the Primary Batter "A" following the directions in Chapter 4. Be sure that you have returned 1 cup of the batter to your sourdough starter container before proceeding with the recipe.

2. Assemble all ingredients and utensils. Let all ingredients come to room temperature.

3. Place the 3 cups of Primary Batter "A" in a large warm bowl. Stir in the 2 cups of warm water, 2 tsp salt and 1 TBS caraway seed.

4. Stir in the 5 cups of rye flour, ½ cup at a time mixing well after each addition.

5. Stir in 1 cup of the white flour. You will have a very stiff but sticky dough.

6. Turn the dough out onto a well floured bread board. Knead in enough additional flour (about 2½ cups) until you have a very stiff dough which will not flatten or spread out.

7. Divide the dough into two parts and form into two round or oblong loaves with the hands. When forming do not break the dough, but just gently stretch it around until it has the shape that you desire. Place on a well greased cookie tin.

8. Cover and place in a warm 85 degree place for proofing. It should proof about 1½ hours, or until almost doubled in bulk.

9. Preheat the oven to 425 degrees and just before baking the bread, put a pan of boiling water in the bottom of the oven. Brush the loaves with cold water and put them into oven to bake. Bake for 45 minutes, removing the pan of boiling water after the first 15 minutes.

10. Place on wire racks to cool.

SOURDOUGH RYE SURPRISE

The dark and light swirls in this bread prove as tasty as they are attractive to look at.

> 3 cups Primary Batter "A"
> 1¾ cups milk
> 2½ cups rye flour
> 1 TBS caraway seed
> 4 tsp salt
> 4 TBS butter
> 4 TBS sugar
> 4½-5 cups white flour

Yield: 2 large loaves

1. Prepare the Primary Batter "A" following the directions in Chapter 4. Be sure that you have returned 1 cup of the batter to your sourdough storage container before proceeding with the recipe.

2. Assemble all ingredients and utensils and let all ingredients come to room temperature.

3. Place 1½ cups of Primary Batter "A" in a large bowl. Stir in 1 cup of milk, 2 TBS sugar, 2 TBS melted butter, 2 tsp salt and 1 TBS caraway seeds.

4. Stir in 2½ cups of rye flour, ½ cup at a time. Turn the dough onto a floured (with white flour) board and knead in enough additional flour to give the dough a smooth and satiny surface.

5. Place the dough in a greased bowl and turn it over. Cover the bowl and set in a warm 85 degree spot until doubled in bulk. This will take slightly over two hours.

6. Immediately (while waiting for the above dough to rise) place 1½ cups of Primary Batter "A" in a large bowl. Stir in ¾ cup of milk, 2 TBS sugar, 2 TBS melted butter and 2 tsp salt.

7. Stir in 2½ cups of white flour, ½ cup at a time, stirring well after each addition.

8. When the dough begins to leave the sides of the bowl turn it onto a floured board and knead until the dough is soft and satiny.

9. Place the dough in a greased bowl, turn it over, cover the bowl and set in a warm 85 degree spot until doubled in bulk. This will take about 2 hours.

10. At the end of the rising period punch each dough ball down and let rise for additional 30 minutes.

11. After proofed for the additional 30 minutes turn out onto a floured board and divide each dough ball into two pieces.

12. With your hands pat one of the rye dough balls out into a rectangle about ½ inch in thickness. Do the same for one of the white dough balls. Place the white dough on top of the rye dough and the with the heel of your hand slightly groove a line in the dough ⅓ of the way from the back of the rectangle. Fold the rear ⅓ of the dough towards yourself and then the front ⅓ of the dough away from yourself over the top of the rest of the dough. Pinch the dough to seal. Repeat this process with the other two pieces of dough.

13. Place the loaves, seam side down, in two well greased loaf pans. Cover the pans and set them in a warm 85 degree spot for 45 minutes or until the dough has doubled in bulk.

14. Bake in a preheated 400 degree oven for 45 minutes or until the dough begins to leave the sides of the pans.

15. When baked remove from pans, brush tops with melted butter and place loaves on their sides on wire rack to cool.

SOURDOUGH BANANA RYE

1½ cups Primary Batter "B"
2 TBS honey
2 cups mashed bananas
3 TBS oil
2 tsp salt
½ tsp baking soda
5-5½ cups rye flour
Yield: 1 round loaf

1 . Prepare the Primary Batter "B" following the directions in Chapter 4. Be sure that you have returned 1 cup of the batter to your starter storage container before adding any ingredients.

2. Assemble all ingredients and utensils. Let all ingredients come to room temperature.

3. Place the 1½ cups of Primary Batter "B" in a 2-quart or larger bowl. Add the 2 TBS of honey and the 2 cups of mashed bananas. Stir well.

4. Stir in the 3 TBS of oil, 2 tsp of salt, ½ tsp baking soda and 2 cups of the rye flour.

5. Add 2½ more cups of rye flour, ½ cup at a time, stirring well. When the dough starts to leave the sides of the bowl turn it out onto a well floured bread board.

6. Knead in the remaining 1 cup of rye flour. You will have a sticky dough. Put the dough in a greased bowl and turn it over. Cover and set in a warm 85 degree place for 2 hours or until doubled in bulk.

7. Punch down and return to the same warm place for an additional 30 minutes.

8. Form one round loaf and place on a greased baking sheet which has been sprinkled with cornmeal. Set in a warm 85 degree place until doubled in bulk again. This will take about 30 minutes.

9. Bake in a preheated 400 degree oven for 45-50 minutes or until the bread sounds hollow when thumped on the bottom.

10. When baked set on a wire rack to cool.

SOURDOUGH PUMPERNICKEL BREAD

1½ cups Primary Batter "B"
1½ cups milk
2 cups whole wheat flour
2 tsp salt
¾ cup cornmeal
2-2½ cups rye flour
Yield: 1 large round loaf.

1. Prepare the Primary Batter "B" following the directions in Chapter 4. Be sure that you have returned one cup of the batter to your sourdough starter container before proceeding with the recipe.

2. Assemble all ingredients and utensils. Let all ingredients come to room temperature.

3. Place the 1½ cups of Primary Batter "B" in a large warm bowl. Stir in the 1½ cups of milk.

4. Stir in the 2 cups of whole wheat flour, ½ cup at a time, stirring after each addition and then stir in the 2 tsp of salt.

5. Stir in the ¾ cup of cornmeal.

6. Stir in 2 cups of the rye flour, ½ cup at a time, stirring after each addition. Stir in enough additional rye flour (about 1 cup) until it is too thick to mix with a spoon.

7. Turn the dough out onto a board floured with rye flour and knead in enough additional rye flour to make a firm dough (about ½ cup).

8. Place in a greased bowl, turn over and cover. Set the bowl in a warm 85 degree spot for 1 hour for proofing.

9. After proofing, turn out and knead for a few seconds to force out pockets of gas and shape into a round loaf. Place on a greased cookie sheet which has been sprinkled with cornmeal. Brush the top with melted cooking oil.

10. Cover and set in a warm 85 degree place for 1 hour more for proofing. Brush the top with cold water just before baking.

11 . Bake in a preheated 375 degree oven for 40 minutes. When done, remove from the oven and place on wire racks to cool.

SOURDOUGH SKILLET CORNBREAD

This cornbread is ideally suited for those who are camping as well as for use at home when there just isn't time to bake something more elaborate. It has a fine, moist crumb and is about the best cornbread the authors have ever eaten.

>   1½ cups Primary Batter "B"
>   1½ cups yellow cornmeal
>   1 cup milk
>   2 eggs
>   2 TBS sugar
>   ¼ cup melted butter
>   ¾ tsp salt
>   ½ tsp baking soda

Yield: 1 10-inch diameter loaf.

1. Prepare the Primary Batter "B" following the directions in Chapter 4. Be sure that you have returned one cup of the batter to your sourdough starter container before proceeding with the recipe.

2. Assemble all ingredients and utensils. Let all ingredients come to room temperature.

3. Put the 1½ cups of Primary Batter "B" in a warm bowl. Stir in the 1½ cups of cornmeal and the 1 cup of milk.

4. Beat the eggs and stir them into the batter. Stir the 2 TBS of sugar in.

5. Melt the ¼ cup of butter and stir it and the ¾ tsp of salt and the ½ tsp of baking soda into the batter.

6. Grease a skillet, or if indoors, a 9-inch greased and floured round cake tin. Turn the batter into the pan and bake in a reflector oven or in your home oven which has been preheated to 450 degrees . Bake for 25 minutes until golden brown on top. Serve hot.

SOURDOUGH CORNMEAL MUFFINS

This recipe makes an exceptional muffin. Just pour the batter into greased muffin tins. Fill each tin ⅔ full. Bake in a preheated 450 degree oven for 20-25 minutes. Even though they are made from the same recipe as the cornbread, they make very high, light muffins.

SOURDOUGH CORNBREAD

This sourdough cornbread is extremely moist and resembles corn-pone of the Southeast in that flour is not added to the bread. The recipe is that of Mrs. Ellen Slutsky of Beverly Hills, California.

    1 cup Room Temperature Sourdough Starter
    1½ cups evaporated milk
    1¾ cups yellow cornmeal
    2 TBS honey
    2 eggs beaten
    ¼ cup oil
    ½ tsp salt
    ½ tsp baking soda
Yield: 1 moist 8 inch square cornbread

1. Prepare the Room Temperature Sourdough Starter following the directions in Chapter 4. Be sure to replenish your original starter before proceeding with the recipe.

2. Assemble all ingredients and utensils. Let all ingredients come to room temperature.

3. Add the 1½ cups of evaporated milk to the 1 cup of sourdough starter.

4. Add the 1¾ cups of yellow cornmeal to the starter and milk and stir well.

5. Add the 2 TBS honey, 2 beaten eggs, ¼ cup oil, ½ tsp salt and ½ tsp baking soda and stir well.

6. Pour batter into a 8 inch square pan and bake in a preheated 400 degree oven for 30 minutes.

7. Serve warm with plenty of butter and honey.

SOURDOUGH CORN FRITTERS

These fritters are perfect with soups and stews of many types. They can also be used as appetizers.

> 1 cup Room Temperature Sourdough Starter
> 1 egg
> 1 cup well drained whole kernel corn
> 1 tsp salt
> ¼ cup melted shortening
> ¾ cup white flour

Yield: About 18 golden corn fritters.

1 . Prepare the Room Temperature Sourdough Starter following the directions in Chapter 4. Be sure to replenish your original starter before proceeding with the recipe.

2. Assemble all ingredients and utensils. Let all ingredients come to room temperature.

3. Beat the egg and add it to the 1 cup of warm sourdough starter.

4. Add the cup of well drained corn, 1 tsp salt and ¼ cup of melted shortening. Stir well.

5. Add the ¾ cup of white flour. A little more or little less flour may be needed. The proper consistency for the batter is when a spoon full of batter is held up it runs off in lengths of about 1½ inches before dropping back into the bowl. Now stir until you have a smooth batter.

6. Cover the batter and set it aside in a warm 85 degree spot for 2 hours.

7 . Drop tablespoonfuls of the batter into deep fat at 380 degrees (use a candy thermometer to determine the temperature). Cook for 2 minutes or until golden brown.

8. Drain and serve immediately.

SOURDOUGH CORNMEAL RAISIN BREAD
(NO-KNEAD)

This bread is really delicious and stays moist for a long time. It's also very good when toasted.

    5 cups Primary Batter "A"
    ⅓ cup melted shortening
    1½ cups milk
    ¾ cup sugar
    1 TBS salt
    2 eggs
    15 drops oil of cinnamon (or 2 tsp ground cinnamon)
    1½ cups yellow cornmeal
    4-4½ cups white flour
    1¼ cups raisins
Yield. 2 large loaves.

1 . Prepare the Primary Batter "A" following the directions in Chapter 4. Be sure that you have returned 1 cup of the batter to your sourdough starter container before proceeding with the recipe.

2. Assemble all ingredients and utensils. Let all ingredients come to room temperature.

3. Melt the ⅓ cup shortening over low heat. Add the 1½ cups milk and heat until lukewarm. Pour into a large warm mixing bowl.

4. Add the ¾ cup sugar, the 1 TBS salt, the 2 eggs beaten, and the 15 drops of cinnamon to the milk and shortening mixture.

5. Stir in the 1½ cups of cornmeal.

6. Stir in the 3 cups of Primary Batter "A"

7. Add 3 cups of the flour, ½ cup at a time, stirring after each addition.

8. Add the 1¼ cups of raisins and the remaining 1½ cups of flour. Mix until all flour is blended in. Batter will be stiff.

9. Cover and set in a warm 85 degree place for proofing until double in size. This will take about 2 hours.

10. Stir the batter down and beat it vigorously for about 30 seconds.

11 . Spread the batter in greased loaf pans, cover the pans, and set in the same warm place until doubled in size or about even with the top of the pans. This will take about 45 minutes.

12. Bake in a preheated 375 degree oven for 45 minutes.

13. Remove from pans when done, brush tops with melted butter and place on wire racks to cool.

SOURDOUGH OATEN-PRUNE BREAD
(NO-KNEAD)

1½ cups Primary Batter "B"
2 cups white flour
¾ cup sugar
½ tsp baking soda
1 tsp salt
1 cup rolled oats
1 cup buttermilk
½ tsp vanilla
2 TBS cooking oil
1 cup diced drained prunes (cooked)
½ cup nut meats (optional)

Yield: 1 loaf.

1. Prepare the Primary Batter "B" following the directions in Chapter 4. Be sure that you have returned 1 cup of the batter to your sourdough starter container before proceeding with the recipe.

2. Assemble all ingredients and utensils. Let all ingredients come to room temperature.

3. Measure the flour. Sift it with the ¾ cup of sugar, the ½ tsp baking soda, and the 1 tsp salt. Stir it into the rolled oats.

4. In a large bowl place the 1 cup of buttermilk. Stir the ½ tsp vanilla, the 2 TBS cooking oil, the 1 cup of diced, drained cooked prunes and the ½ cup of nut meats into the milk.

5. Stir the 1½ cups of Primary Batter "B" into the milk and prune mixture.

6. Add the flour mixture all at once and stir only until the flour is dampened.

7. Put the dough into a well greased loaf pan, cover, and set in a warm 85 degree place for 15 minutes for proofing.

8. Bake in a preheated 350-375 degree oven for 1 hour.

9. Remove from oven and remove the loaf from the pan. Place it on a wire rack to cool.

SOURDOUGH OATEN-DATE BREAD

The above recipe lends itself very well to adaptation by substituting 1 cup of diced dates for the prunes. It makes a delicious loaf.

SOURDOUGH OATMEAL RAISIN BANNOCKS

1 cup Room Temperature Sourdough Starter
2 TBS sugar
½ tsp salt
1 tsp baking soda
¼ cup butter
2 eggs beaten
½ cup chopped raisins
1 cup rolled oats
¾ cup white flour
Yield: 8 bannocks

1 . Prepare the Room Temperature Sourdough Starter following the directions in Chapter 4. Be sure to replenish your original starter before proceeding with the recipe.

2. Assemble all ingredients and utensils. Let all ingredients come to room temperature.

3. Place the 1 cup of sourdough starter at room temperature in a 2-quart or larger bowl. Stir in 2 TBS sugar, ½ tsp salt, 1 tsp baking soda.

4. Melt the ¼ cup or butter and let cool to lukewarm. Stir it into the batter.

5. Beat 2 eggs. Measure out 2 TBS of egg and save for later. Stir the rest into the batter.

6. Stir ½ cup of finely chopped or cut raisins into the batter followed by 1 cup of rolled oats. Stir in ¾ cup white flour.

7. Turn onto a floured bread board and knead just enough to cause the dough to hold together. Divide the dough in two pieces and pat each one out to a thickness of ½ inch, and in a circular shape. This is a soft dough. Each piece of dough is a bannock.

8. Grease a cookie tin or baking sheet and then brush the tops of each bannock with some of the egg saved previously. Turn them over and place on the baking tin. Brush the top side now with egg.

9. Cover the pan with a cloth supported by two water tumblers and let rest in a warm 85 degree spot for 1 hour.

10. With a sharp knife divide each bannock into quarters by cutting about half way through the dough. Do not cut completely through.

11 . Bake in a preheated 400 degree oven for 15-20 minutes or until brown.

12. Serve warm for breakfast or tea.

SOURDOUGH BUCKWHEAT BREAD

1½ cups Primary Batter "B"
1 cup milk
½ tsp ginger
¼ cup molasses
2 cups buckwheat flour
4 TBS melted butter
1½ tsp salt
2-2½ cups white flour

Yield: 2 dark loaves.

1 . Prepare the Primary Batter "B" following the directions in Chapter 4. Be sure that you have returned 1 cup of the batter to your sourdough starter container before adding other ingredients.

2. Assemble all ingredients and utensils. Let all ingredients come to room temperature.

3. Place the 1½ cups of Primary Batter "B" in a warm bowl. Stir in the 1 cup of milk which has been brought to room temperature.

4. Add the ½ tsp ginger and the ¼ cup of molasses and stir well.

5. Add the 2 cups of buckwheat flour, ½ cup at a time, stirring after each addition.

6. Stir in the 4 TBS of melted butter and the 1½ tsp of salt. Stir in 1½ cups of the white flour. .

7. Spread the remaining 1 cup of white flour on a board and turn the dough out onto it. Knead in enough of this flour to make a smooth and non-sticky dough.

8. Place dough in a greased bowl, turn it over, cover it and set the bowl in a warm 85 degree spot for proofing for 1½ hours or until doubled in bulk.

9. When doubled in bulk turn out onto a board and shape into 2 loaves with generously floured hands. Place these loaves in well greased loaf pans with the ends of the loaves just touching the ends of the pans. Cover the pans and set them in a warm place for proofing for 1½ hours.

10. Bake in a preheated 375 degree oven for 40 minutes. When done, remove from pans and place on wire racks to cool.

SOURDOUGH BOSTON BROWN BREAD

Here is an adaptation of the traditional dark steamed bread eaten so often with baked beans.

1 cup Room Temperature Sourdough Starter
1 cup rye flour
1 cup graham flour
1 cup yellow cornmeal
2 tsp baking soda
1 tsp salt
1 cup buttermilk
¾ cup unsulphured molasses
1 cup raisins

Yield: 2 1-quart loaves or 2 1-pound loaves

1 . Prepare the Room Temperature Sourdough Starter following the directions in Chapter 4. Be sure to replenish your original starter before proceeding with the recipe.

2. Assemble all ingredients and utensils. Let all ingredients come to room temperature.

3. In a 2-quart or larger bowl stir together 1 cup rye flour, 1 cup graham flour, 1 cup yellow cornmeal, 2 tsp baking soda and 1 tsp salt.

4. In another bowl stir together 1 cup of sourdough starter, 1 cup buttermilk and ¾ cup unsulphured molasses.

5. Add the raisins to the flour mixture and stir lightly. Make a well in the flour mixture and pour in the starter-buttermilk mixture. Stir thoroughly.

6. Grease two number 2 cans (these cans usually contain about 1¼ pounds of canned fruit). Pour the batter into the cans. They should be about ⅔ full.

7. Cover the cans with two layers of foil or wax paper and fasten with a rubber band. It is important that the cans be covered to prevent steam from condensing on the inside of the pan lid and then dropping onto the bread.

8. Put the cans on a trivet in a large pan which has a cover. Pour boiling water into the pan until it reaches halfway up the sides of the cans. Cover the pan and steam the bread for 3 hours.

9. Remove the cans from the boiling water and place in a 400 degree oven for 15 minutes.

10. Remove from the cans by opening the other end and pushing the bread out. If serving immediately cut with a piece of string as the bread is too moist to cut properly with a knife.

11 . Although usually served with baked beans this bread also is a great snack or tea bread when sliced thin. Cheese spreads are ideal on it.

Chapter 9
Sourdough French Bread

Sourdough French Bread is the only truly American bread to rank with the great breads of the world. While we in the United States have contributed many other breads and all the cornbreads, it is only San Francisco Sourdough French Bread that has captured the imagination and love that are part of a great bread. Like any great bread, it has an aura or mystique surrounding its origins and baking. Much of this is justly deserved. Here we shall attempt to give you the background of this bread and to give you recipes which will allow you to bake a fine loaf of bread.

San Francisco Sourdough French Bread was an adaptation of ordinary French bread to the conditions and ingredients available. Today it has evolved to a point where it stands alone in its own light rather than being considered a variation of another bread. Almost everyone who has been to San Francisco has tasted this unique bread and most have fallen in love with it. Many carry loaves of it back home with them by plane when leaving. Many others want to know how to bake the same bread in their own kitchens. You will never get the same bread as is baked in San Francisco for a myriad of reasons. The main reason is that your oven cannot be made into a commercial oven. However, this chapter will give you some clues on how to come as close as is reasonably possible without building your own commercial oven.

The first point to make is that French bread is baked by many recipes. The ordinary household in France does not bake bread. It is all commercially baked by men who have had long years of training and apprenticeship. Why struggle to bake your own bread when someone with the training, skills and equipment can do it for much less cost and with superior results. French bread as baked in France is limited to four ingredients: flour, water, salt, and yeast. It is this yeast which differentiates their bread from that baked in San Francisco. The French use commercial yeast rather than sourdough. Before the advent of commercial yeast, they used a principle similar to that we employ here in the book. From each day's baking a small amount of the dough containing the yeast was saved.

This was multiplied about the same way that we set a Primary Batter here in this book. The major difference was that at no time was any yeast allowed to go beyond the multiplication point to the stage where the yeast would begin to ferment the flour and water mixture. Today's commercial yeasts will ferment if given enough time and a warm place, but will not approximate the quality from a good sourdough starter. A good sourdough starter has a different form of the yeast microorganism which, while acting more slowly, also produces a much stronger fermentation action. Thus, the French used to bake with a starter but not a sourdough starter. In fact, the proofing temperatures used by the French are generally quite low in order to prevent fermentation. It is our particular form of starter which gives the San Francisco Sourdough French Bread its particular goodness.

San Francisco Sourdough French Bread is also baked in special ovens. It is these ovens which cause the bread to have its characteristic chewy crust and its moist insides. These ovens have elaborate steam injection devices.

While these are formidable obstacles to overcome, there are methods which you can use to produce a reasonable facsimile of the real thing. By following the directions for baking bread in this chapter, you can produce a fine loaf of bread which few will be able to differentiate from the real thing. Only a native San Franciscan will be able to tell that your bread was produced in your kitchen at home rather than flown directly from San Francisco.

These recipes are arranged in ascending order of difficulty and complexity. The first one will give you a good loaf of Sourdough French Bread that requires less effort than the Sourdough White Bread 1 recipe in Chapter 7 . Many will be satisfied with this bread. If you are a perfectionist, you will want to try all the steps included in the following recipes to bake an even more delicious and perfect loaf. Some of these require more time and effort, but you will be rewarded with a superior product. Since each recipe assumes knowledge acquired in the ones preceding it you are advised to attempt them in order. Ideally, each recipe should be baked several times before proceeding to the next one, so that all the techniques have been well learned. Beginning with the most difficult recipe may lead to problems if all the knowledge contained in the previous recipes is not properly put to use.

The bread is baked on a flat stone surface and is covered with the mist injected by the steam devices during the first few minutes of baking. To get your oven to approximate these conditions takes some energy, initiative, and work. Even then, you can expect only an approximation. Remember that in San Francisco the bread is being baked by professionals who spend their whole day (and night) baking the bread and thus know exactly what to do at each step of preparation and baking, plus also what to do to rectify anything which is not correct at any point in the operation. In reality it is these men, using a carefully controlled starter, who bake this great bread. Remember that even with all the correct equipment you will never have the experience that they do and so do not be disappointed if that certain something from San Francisco seems lacking. It is not the famous and beautiful San Francisco fog or the ocean air or the type of flour or any secret unlisted ingredients, but the men themselves, their ovens and a well cared for starter that produce this bread.

SOURDOUGH FRENCH BREAD I

1½ cups Primary Batter "B"
1 cup warm water
2 tsp salt
4 cups flour
Yield: 2 loaves.

1 . Prepare the Primary Batter "B" following the directions in Chapter 4. Be sure that you have returned 1 cup of the batter to your sourdough starter container before continuing with the recipe.

2. Assemble all ingredients and utensils. Let all ingredients come to room temperature. The importance of room temperature for the ingredients cannot be stressed enough. It is one of the most usual causes for failure.

3. Put the 1½ cups of Primary Batter "B" in a large warm bowl.

4. Stir in the cup of water. The ideal temperature for this water is 90 degrees. Do not add the water if it is hotter than 95 degrees or you will risk killing the sourdough and then your bread will not rise.

5. Stir in 1 cup of the flour, then sprinkle the salt on top of the batter.

6. Stir in enough additional flour, ½ cup at a time, stirring after each addition and scraping down the sides of the bowl until the dough leaves the sides of the bowl. This will take approximately 2-2¼ more cups.

7. Turn the dough out onto a well floured board and knead in enough additional flour (about ½-¾ cup) to make the dough just smooth and elastic. The dough should be softer than when making the Sourdough White Bread 1 recipe.

8. Put the dough in warm bowl at least 4 quarts in size and cover securely with plastic wrap. Since this bread is not covered with a layer of oil it will dry out if you don't do this. The ideal bowl for this proofing should be steep sided to help the dough rise better.

9. This bowl should be placed in a warm 85 degree place for proofing. The importance of this temperature has been stressed before, but it is essential to good bread when baking with sourdough. The dough should proof for approximately 2 hours or until it has doubled in bulk.

10. When the dough has doubled in bulk, turn it out onto a lightly floured bread board and knead it for 30 seconds. Divide it into 2 pieces with a sharp knife. Fold in half lengthwise. Cover with waxed paper and let rest 5 minutes on back of board.

11. Shape each piece into a loaf by patting it out with your hands into a large oval which is about 1-1½ inches thick. Fold the dough in half from the back to the front. Pinch the near edge to seal. Then roll the dough part way around so the pinched seal is on top. Flatten the dough again with your hand and using the side of your hand press a trench lengthwise down the center of the oval. Fold the back half forward again and once again pinch the edges together. Then roll the dough back and forth with the palms of your hand lengthening it until it has reached a length about 2 inches shorter than the sheet on which you will bake it. This sheet should be almost as big as your oven. There should be about 2 inches around all sides of the sheet between it and the oven walls.

12. When the loaves are the correct size, place them on a greased cookie sheet which has been sprinkled with white cornmeal. If you are out of cornmeal, place some uncooked spaghetti in a blender and grind it until it is the size of coarse cornmeal. Each loaf should have the seam side down and they should be at least three inches apart.

13. Cover, using a pair of water tumblers or bent hangers to keep the cloth from touching the loaves. Set in a warm 85 degree spot until the loaves have doubled in bulk again. This will take approximately 1 hour. The loaves are ready for baking when the imprint of two fingers pushed about ½ inch into the dough remains.

Form the loaf

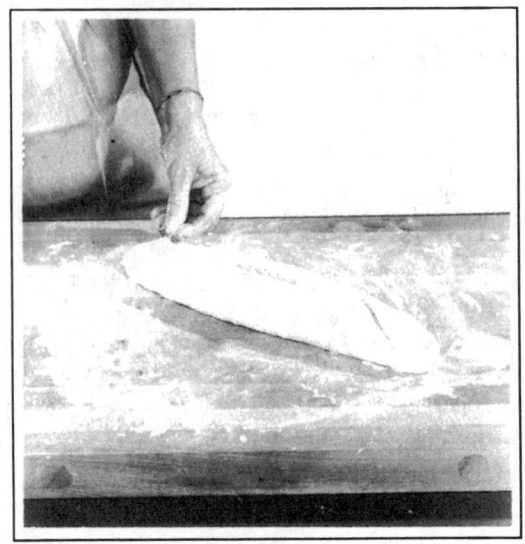

Slash the loaf

14. Using an extremely sharp knife or a razor blade, make three slashes in the top of each loaf. These slashes should be cut to a depth of ¼-½ inch and should be as close to parallel with the surface of the bread as possible. The slashes break the carefully constructed gluten structure on the surface of the loaf and cause the bread to develop that rough look when baking as the bread swells up through them. After slashing, brush the loaves with cold water to give the crusts the proper color and texture.

15. The oven should be preheated to 400 degrees and just before putting the bread in the oven, set a tin pan with boiling water in it on the bottom of the oven. This is important to develop the proper crust. It helps to approximate the steam injection in the ovens in the San Francisco bakeries.

16. Put the sheet with the loaves on it in the oven. It should be slightly above the center of the oven, but not in the top third of the oven.

17. After 10 minutes of baking, remove the pan of water from the oven. Continue baking the bread for an additional 35 minutes or until the crust is browned.

18. Remove from the oven and place on wire racks to cool. Brush immediately with cold water to add sheen to the crust. Remember that although the aroma is delicious the bread really tastes better when cool as then the inside has had a chance to set. Warm bread seems to taste great, but the real test is when the bread has cooled, as then it is really completed. Eating the bread before it has thoroughly cooled is similar to eating anything before it is completely cooked. You have not let the baking be completely finished.

SOURDOUGH FRENCH BREAD II

This recipe includes an extra proofing period and more details on how to make a better bread. Notice that it uses the same ingredients in the same amounts as the first recipe. The difference in your bread is due to this additional proofing period, plus a slightly different method of proofing for the shaped loaves.

> 1½ cups Primary Batter "B"
> 1 cup warm water
> 2 tsp salt
> 4 cups flour

Yield: 2 loaves.

1. Prepare the Primary Batter "B" following the directions in Chapter 4. Be sure that you have returned 1 cup of the batter to your sourdough starter container before continuing with the recipe.

2. Assemble all ingredients and utensils. Let all ingredients come to room temperature.

3. Put the 1½ cups of Primary Batter "B" in a large warm bowl.

4. Stir in the cup of warm water. This water should be at 90 degrees.

5. Stir in 1 cup of the flour and then sprinkle the salt on top of the batter.

6. Stir in enough additional flour, ½ cup at a time, stirring after each addition, to make the dough leave the sides of the bowl. This takes approximately 2 more cups.

7. Turn the dough out onto a well floured board and knead in enough additional flour to make the dough smooth and elastic. This takes about ¾-1 cup more.

8. Put the dough in a warm bowl at least 4 quarts in size. Cover securely with plastic wrap.

9. Set the bowl in a warm 85 degree place for proofing. The dough should proof until doubled in bulk. This takes approximately 2 hours.

10. When doubled in bulk, punch down with your fist once. Fold the edges over into the impression left by the fist and turn the dough over. Seal tightly again and let proof at 85 degrees for an additional 1½ hours or until doubled in bulk again.

11 . When doubled in bulk the second time turn the dough out onto a lightly floured board and knead it for 30 seconds. Divide it into two pieces with a sharp knife.

12. Shape each loaf following the directions in the Sourdough French Bread I recipe.

13. When the loaves are shaped, place them on a cloth covered board or pan which has cornmeal sprinkled on it and cover so that the cloth is not touching the loaves. In this case, place the loaves with the seam side up, rather than down.

14. Let the loaves proof again until doubled in bulk. This will take about 1 hour.

15. When proofed properly, take a stiff piece of cardboard or a thin sheet of plywood and gently and carefully roll one loaf off of the proofing board or pan and onto the cardboard or plywood. Gently transfer the loaf onto a greased pan which has been sprinkled with white cornmeal. Be careful to keep the seam side down. This requires sliding the loaf rather than rolling it during this operation. Remember to use as gentle and light a touch as possible during this operation to prevent the structure of the bread from being disturbed.

16. Again, slash the tops and brush with cold water as in the first recipe. The position of the three slashes is critical to a better looking loaf. It does not make any difference in the taste however. The first slash should be parallel with the direction of the loaf and directly in the center of the far end. It should start about 1 inch from the far end of the loaf and come approximately ⅓ the length of the loaf. The second slash should be diagonal starting about 1 or 2 inches further back from the near end of the first slash and about 1 or 2 inches to the right of center. It should also be about ⅓ the length of the loaf and should end up on the left side of the loaf. The third slash should be identical to the first, except that it is at the near end of the bread. Repeat the process with the second loaf.

17. Place the cookie sheet in a preheated 400 degree oven with a pan of boiling water in the bottom. After five minutes, brush the loaves with cold water. If brushing the loaves in a hot oven is difficult, or you have very sensitive hands you can use an atomizer to cover the loaves with cold water. A thoroughly cleaned bottle with a push atomizer, such as window cleaner bottles, is perfect. Close the oven door and after a second five minutes, brush again with cold water. Repeat this process once more after another five minutes. At this time, remove the pan of boiling water from the oven. Continue baking for an additional 30 minutes or until brown. This is a total baking time of 45 minutes.

18. Remove from sheet and place on wire racks to cool.

SOURDOUGH FRENCH BREAD III

This recipe will produce a loaf of Sourdough French Bread which is as close to that baked by the famous San Franciscan bakeries as can be produced in your own kitchen. It requires the investment of a few dollars for equipment and materials to help simulate the actual situation under which the bread is baked in San Francisco. It requires more patience and also requires some practice as both the equipment that you use to handle the shaped loaves and the cooking surfaces are different.

The major problem in attempting to recreate the commercial ovens is the cooking surface. The bakeries do not use any sort of pans or sheets to bake their bread on. They bake the bread directly on stone hearths in the ovens. To come as close as is feasible without spending a fortune one can attempt only to recreate the baking surface. To do this, measure the size of your oven. Go to your nearest building supply dealer and ask for either quarry tile or a piece of asbestos cement. Both will work fine. Have the asbestos cement cut to a size of 1 inch smaller than the size of a shelf in your oven. For this purpose the asbestos cement should be ¼ inch thick. If you are buying quarry tile, buy enough to give you the same coverage. It should not cost you more than $2-4. This surface should be set on a rack in your oven prior to preheating the oven. It should be slightly higher than the middle of your oven, but not in the top third.

The additional equipment needed is a pastry cloth and something which can be used as a bread paddle. To put the loaves onto this surface and to remove them when they are done, a paddle is necessary. You can buy a commercial one in restaurant supply houses or you can make your own by fastening a ¼ inch thick piece of highest grade plywood onto a handle. It should be very securely fastened as the act of removing the paddle from under the loaves when they are in the oven is critical.

Now that you have provided yourself with these items on with the baking. Once again you will use the same ingredients and the same procedures you have used up to now. There will be the additional procedures associated with the special cooking surface which are described in the greatest detail. Do not overlook any of the precautions or steps taken previously or you risk a less than ideal loaf of bread.

> 1½ cups Primary Batter "B"
> 1 cup warm water
> 2 tsp salt
> 4 cups flour

Yield. 2 loaves.

1. Prepare the Primary Batter "B" following the directions in Chapter 4. Be sure that you have returned 1 cup of the batter to your sourdough starter container before proceeding with the recipe.

2. Assemble all ingredients and utensils. Let all ingredients come to room temperature.

3. Put the 1½ cups of Primary Batter "B" in a large warm bowl.

4. Stir in the 1 cup of warm water at 90 degrees.

5. Stir in 1 cup of the flour, ½ cup at a time, and then sprinkle the 2 tsp of salt on the top of the batter.

6. Stir in enough additional flour (about 2 cups) to make the dough leave the sides of the bowl.

7. Turn the dough onto a well floured board and knead in enough additional flour to make the dough smooth and elastic. This will take approximately ¾-1 cup more.

8. Put the dough in a warm bowl of at least 4-quart capacity. Cover securely with plastic wrap.

9. Set the bowl in a warm 85 degree place for proofing. When the dough has doubled in bulk, which takes about 2 hours, the proofing is over.

10. Punch down the dough and fold the edges over the impression left by the fist. Turn the dough over and recover the bowl. Place it again in a warm 85 degree spot for proofing for an additional 1½ hours or until doubled in bulk again.

11. Turn the dough out onto a floured board and shape into loaves as in the previous recipes. When each loaf is shaped, carefully place it on a board or pastry cloth as in the preceding recipe. The seam should be up. The pastry cloth should have flour rubbed vigorously into it and then should be sprinkled with white cornmeal. Cover the loaves, being careful not to let the cloth touch the loaves. Set them in a warm 85 degree spot until they double in bulk. This will take about 1 hour.

12. When proofed properly the bread has to be placed on the paddle to be ready to be placed in the oven. This should be done by gently rolling a loaf on to the paddle which has been heavily sprinkled with white corn-meal. Now the seam should be down. Do this to the second loaf so that now you have the loaves both on the paddle and about 3 inches apart.

13. Now brush the loaves with cold water and slash them following the procedures in the previous recipes.

14. You have by now also placed the tiles or asbestos in the oven and preheated it to 400 degrees. You have also placed a pan of boiling water in the floor of the oven and are now ready to slide the loaves off the paddle onto the hot surface.

15. Place the paddle in the oven so that the far end of the paddle is at the far end of the tile or asbestos. Now with a quick but smooth jerk remove the paddle from under the loaves of bread. If you have never done this before, it can be tricky. You are urged to experiment with a loaf of soft bread or even with a properly shaped loaf of bread in a cold oven to perfect the technique of removing the loaves from the paddle without causing them to be misshapen or to be wrinkled. The hot tile or asbestos will cause the loaves to stick to it for the first few minutes of baking. There can be no rearranging of the bread once it has touched the surface. When you feel sure of your technique then go ahead and use this recipe.

16. Following the directions in the preceding recipe brush with cold water every 5 minutes for the first 15 minutes and remove the pan of boiling water when the first 15 minutes are up. Bake for an additional 30 minutes or until brown. Remove with the paddle and place on a wire rack to cool.

17. When the oven is cool, remove the tiles or asbestos and brush with a stiff brush to remove any particles which might soil. Clean your pastry canvas thoroughly and store all for the next baking.

SOURDOUGH FRENCH ROLLS I

> 1½ cups Primary Batter "B"
> 1 cup warm water
> 2 tsp salt
> 4 cups flour

Yield: 20 rolls.

1. Prepare the Primary Batter "B" following the directions in Chapter 4. Be sure that you have returned 1 cup of the batter to your sourdough starter container before continuing with the recipe.

2. Assemble all ingredients and utensils. Let all ingredients come to room temperature. The importance of room temperature for the ingredients cannot be stressed enough. It is one of the most usual causes for failure.

3. Put the 1½ cups of Primary Batter "B" in a large warm bowl.

4. Stir in the 1 cup of water. The ideal temperature for this water is 90 degrees. Do not add the water if it is hotter than 95 degrees or you will risk killing the sourdough and then your bread will not rise.

5. Stir in 1 cup of the flour, then sprinkle the salt on top of the batter.

6. Stir in enough additional flour, ½ cup at a time, stirring after each addition and scraping down the sides of the bowl until the dough leaves the sides of the bowl. This will take approximately 2-2¼ more cups.

7. Turn the dough out onto a well floured board and knead in enough additional flour (about ½-¾ cup) to make the dough just smooth and elastic. The dough should be softer than when making the Sourdough White Bread 1 recipe.

8. Put the dough in a warm bowl at least 4 quarts in size and cover securely with plastic wrap. Since this dough is not covered with a layer of oil it will dry out if you don't do this. The ideal bowl for this proofing should be steep sided to help the dough rise better.

9. This bowl should be placed in a warm 85 degree place for proofing. The importance of this temperature has been stressed before, but it is essential to good bread when baking with sourdough. The dough should proof for approximately 2 hours or until it has doubled in bulk.

10. When the dough has doubled in bulk turn it out onto a lightly floured board and knead it for 30 seconds. Then pat it out with the palm of your hand until it is a large rectangle and about 1½ inches thick. Take a sharp knife and cut the dough into approximately 20 pieces each about 4 inches square.

11 . Separate the cut pieces and fold each piece over itself and seal the edges by pinching. Place the rolls on a well greased cookie sheet which has been sprinkled with white cornmeal. The rolls can be placed in rows about 3 inches apart with the ends about 1 inch apart if you want the type of french rolls which make good sandwiches or with the ends about 3 inches apart if you want the rolls to have more rounded ends.

12. Cover the rolls with a cloth which is kept from touching the rolls by tumblers or other means and set the sheet in a warm 85 degree place until the rolls have doubled in bulk. Again, if the impression of two fingers pressed about ½ inch into the dough remains then the dough is ready for baking. This should take approximately 1 hour.

13 . Just before baking slash each roll once with a razor blade or extremely sharp knife. This slash should be cut as close to parallel to the surface of the roll as possible. It should run lengthwise. It can be either diagonal or straight, depending on your preference. Brush the rolls with cold water.

14. Place a pan of boiling water on the floor of the preheated 400 degree oven just before putting the rolls in to bake.

15. Bake the rolls for 15 minutes then remove the pan of boiling water and continue to bake for an additional 30 minutes or until the rolls are brown.

16. Remove from the oven and place on wire racks to cool.

SOURDOUGH FRENCH ROLLS II

This recipe is identical to the Sourdough French Bread II recipe up to the shaping of the loaves. Shape the loaves in the same manner as you did for the Sourdough French Roll 1 recipe. This recipe therefore has given the dough an additional proofing period. It is this that gives your rolls a stronger flavor and better texture. After shaping the rolls, place them on a greased cookie sheet which has been sprinkled with cornmeal. Cover, being sure that the cloth does not touch the rolls and put in a warm 85 degree spot to rise. When doubled in bulk, which takes approximately 1 hour, brush with cold water and slash the tops as you did in the first french roll recipe. Follow the directions for baking Sourdough French Bread II to bake these rolls in Steps 17 and 18.

SOURDOUGH FRENCH ROLLS III

This recipe is identical to the Sourdough French Roll II recipe except that after forming the rolls and letting them proof they are slipped onto the hot asbestos or tile from the paddle. They are removed the same way. You will find that this gives the rolls the authentic taste that is desired.

SOURDOUGH WHOLE WHEAT
FRENCH BREAD AND ROLLS

Sourdough whole wheat french bread and rolls are not part of the San Francisco sourdough heritage. However, these delicious products are made by the same methods.

All of the recipes in this chapter can be converted to whole wheat simply by substituting 2 cups of whole wheat flour for 2 cups of the white flour. Make the whole wheat flour the first to be added and finish up with the 2 cups of white flour. All other procedures and techniques are the same. The only difference is that when proofing the bread may not actually double in size. However, the same proofing periods are needed.

A final word is in order at this point. Do not be discouraged if you have baked a less than perfect bread. The techniques are different and there are many new steps to be perfected. In time you will be producing great loaves of bread. This bread is one of the most demanding and difficult breads to make because of high standards which have been set by the bakeries in San Francisco. Remember that much training and a lot of specialized equipment is used to bake the bread that you buy on Fisherman's Wharf or eat in the restaurants here. There are some steps which can be taken to correct problems. Probably the most common cause of problems is failure to have all ingredients and utensils at room temperature or slightly higher and to insure that the proofing is done in a warm enough spot. When you have these items under control the next most common problem is an oven which does not have an accurate thermostat. Use a high quality oven thermometer to check this.

For specific problems also check the following items. If your crust is not brown and the above items relating to temperature were followed then you may need more salt. The next time you bake add ½ tsp more salt. If your crust is too brown then take the pan of boiling water out of the oven after the first 10 minutes rather than after 15 minutes. If the crust is too tough then your kitchen was too humid and the outside of the dough formed into a permanent texture earlier than it was supposed to. Or else the weather may have been too damp. Try again with less humidity. If the bread did not rise enough after being placed in the oven you let it rise until it was past the doubled in bulk stage in the final proofing before baking. Be more careful the next time as the sourdough already used all its leavening power before the baking under those conditions. If the bread is heavy or it hasn't the proper amount of holes inside, then you haven't let the dough proof enough or it hasn't proofed at the right temperature. In this case you have not sufficiently activated the powers of the sourdough. If you desire more bubbles in your bread, be extremely gentle while forming the loaves and if you feel that fewer bubbles are to be desired then knead the bread gently but firmly for about 30 seconds being careful not to cause the surface to break.

Many people like round loaves of Sourdough French Bread. Following the recipes in this chapter will give you excellent bread which can also be formed into round loaves. When forming the loaves, be careful not to tear the surface of the dough. Stretch and pull the dough until it is molded into the correct round shape. The only other modification is to slash the bread in a different manner. The slashes should be made to a depth of about ¼ inch and should be perpendicular to the surface of the dough. There should be four slashes which form a square inscribed on the top of the loaf and slightly smaller than the loaf. Baking time and temperature remains the same.

Chapter 10
Breads of Other Lands

This chapter contains recipes for breads which are identified with specific foreign countries. Some are breads which are baked at holiday times, some are breakfast breads and yet others are the everyday breads of the people. We have experimented extensively with sourdough in these breads. The results are the following recipes which embody sourdough in the traditional breads of other countries. All of these recipes produce extremely good results that are varied in taste, texture and shape. You can be assured of many compliments when you bake these recipes. For an adventure in baking and eating with an international flare don't miss any of these recipes.

SOURDOUGH BAGELS

1½ cups Primary Batter "B"
1¾ cups flour
1 tsp salt
3 TBS sugar
3 TBS salad oil
2 eggs
2 TBS sugar in 4 quarts boiling water
Yield: 12-14 bagels.

1 . Prepare the Primary Batter following the directions in Chapter 4. Be sure that you have returned 1 cup of the batter to your sourdough starter container before proceeding with the recipe.

2. Assemble all ingredients and utensils. Let all ingredients come to room temperature.

3. Sift 1½ cups of the flour, 1 tsp salt and 3 TBS sugar into a warm bowl. Stir in the 3 TBS salad oil and the 2 eggs.

4. Stir in the 1½ cups of Primary Batter "B" and add enough additional flour for the dough to leave the sides of the bowl.

5. Turn the dough onto a well floured board and knead in enough additional flour to make the dough smooth and elastic (about ¼ cup).

6. Place in a warm greased bowl, cover and set the bowl in a warm 85 degree spot until doubled in bulk. This will take about 2 hours. When doubled, punch down and let proof for an additional 1½ hours or until doubled in bulk.

7. Turn the dough out onto a floured board and divide it into 12-14 equal pieces. Roll each piece into a 6-inch roll and about ¾ inch thick. Pinch the two ends together to form a doughnut shape.

8. Boil the 4 quarts of water and add the 2 TBS of sugar. Drop each bagel into the boiling water one at a time. Boil only 4 at a time. Cook until they rise to the top of the water and then turn over and cook for two minutes longer.

9. Remove with a slotted spoon and place on a greased cookie sheet. When all have been boiled and placed on the cookie sheet, put in a preheated 375 degree oven and bake for 20-25 minutes until crusty and golden brown.

10. Serve with lox and cream cheese or your favorite sandwich filling.

SOURDOUGH ENGLISH MUFFINS

1½ cups Primary Batter "B"
1½ cups flour
1 TBS sugar
1 tsp salt
½ tsp baking soda
Yield: about 10 3-inch muffins.

1 . Prepare the Primary Batter "B" following the directions in Chapter 4. Be sure that you have returned 1 cup of the batter to your sourdough starter container before continuing with the recipe.

2. Assemble all ingredients and utensils. Let all ingredients come to room temperature.

3. Put the 1½ cups of Primary Batter "B" in a warm 4-quart bowl.

4. Stir in the ½ tsp soda and 1 TBS of sugar and the 1 tsp of salt. Add 1¼ cups of flour in small amounts at a time.

5. Turn this dough out onto a board floured with the remaining ¼ cup of flour. Knead this dough until it is no longer sticky. About 2-3 minutes. Add flour if necessary.

6. Roll the dough out to a thickness of ½ inch. Using a 3-inch cutter cut out 10 muffins. An empty can works fine, if you don't have a 3-inch cutter.

7. Place the muffins about 1 inch apart on a cookie tin which has been sprinkled with cornmeal. Put the tin in a warm 85 degree place for 45 minutes for proofing.

8. Preheat an electric griddle to 325 degrees, or a frying pan over a medium flame. Cook the muffins for 10 minutes on each side in the lightly greased pan.

9. Serve hot. They can be cooled and later split and toasted.

SOURDOUGH CRUMPETS

1½ cups Primary Batter "B"
¾ tsp salt
½ cup milk
½ cup flour
Yield: about 6 crumpets.

1. Prepare the Primary Batter "B" following the directions in Chapter 4. Before adding other ingredients, be sure that you have returned 1 cup of your batter to your sourdough starter container.

2. Assemble all ingredients and utensils. Let all ingredients come to room temperature.

3. Put the 1½ cups of Primary Batter "B" in a warm bowl.

4. Stir in the ½ cup of milk, the ¾ tsp of salt, and the ½ cup flour.

5. You will have a very thin batter. Using a wooden spoon, beat the batter for three minutes.

6. Cover the bowl and put in a warm 85 degree place for 30 minutes.

7. Beat with a wooden spoon again for three minutes and recover and replace in the same warm place for 30 minutes longer.

8. Repeat Step 7 once more.

9. Over a medium flame place a greased frying pan with six crumpet rings in it. When hot beat the batter for a short period of time and pour it into the rings until each one is ⅓ full. If you don't have crumpet rings the cans that tuna fish come in work fine. Just remove the tops and bottoms, scrub thoroughly and grease before placing in the frying pan. Use only cans without any manufacturers' lining or glaze or your crumpets will stick.

10. Cook until the surface is dry and the bottom is brown. Remove the rings and using a pancake turner turn the crumpets and brown the second side lightly.

11. Cool on a wire rack.

12. To serve, toast the crumpets and serve with plenty of butter and jam.

SOURDOUGH PEDA
(SOURDOUGH ARMENIAN BREAD)

These small loaves have a hollow center which just begs to be filled with grated cheese, cooked ground beef or pork, chili, or even a thick stew. These are also good when reheated.

1½ cups Primary Batter "B"
7 cups flour
1 TBS salt
2 TBS sugar
1½ cups warm water

Yield. 12 small crusty loaves about the size of extra large hamburger buns.

1. Prepare the Primary Batter "B" following the directions in Chapter 4. Be sure that you have returned 1 cup of the batter to your sourdough starter container before continuing with the recipe.

2. Assemble all ingredients and utensils. Let all ingredients come to room temperature.

3. Sift the 7 cups of flour, 1 TBS of salt and 2 TBS of sugar into a large bowl.

4. Stir in the 1½ cups of Primary Batter "B" followed by the 1½ cups of warm water. With wooden spoon stir slowly (just in the middle of the bowl) to mix batter with flour to consistency to knead.

5. Knead in the bowl, adding more flour or water to bring the dough to a smooth firm texture which is not stiff. Do not add over 6 additional TBS water.

6. Brush the top with butter, cover and set in a warm 85 degree spot for proofing. The dough should proof until it has doubled in bulk which should be about 2 hours.

7. Punch the dough down and then turn it out onto a floured board. Divide the dough into 12 pieces.

8. Shape the pieces into balls and let rest covered for 10 minutes.

9. Prepare the oven by removing the racks and preheating it to 450 degrees.

10. When the oven is hot, take 1 to 4 balls and pat them each to a thickness of about ¼ inch. Make certain that there are not creases or folds in the dough.

11. Using a wooden paddle slide the loaves directly onto the floor of the oven. Bake for 10 minutes or until the tops are browned. Repeat for the remaining balls of dough.

12. If loaves tend to bum on the bottom before they are brown on top, bake only until they are done. Then brown the tops under the broiler.

13. Only serve hot. These loaves keep well and can be easily reheated.

If you have gone to the expense of buying quarry tiles to put in your oven to make a better surface on which to bake french bread, then you can obtain superlative results with this recipe by putting them on the bottom of the oven as it is heating. Bake the peda on this surface. Be sure your tiles and oven are heated to proper temperature (450 degrees) before trying to bake the peda.

SOURDOUGH ENSAIMADE
(SOURDOUGH SPANISH COFFEECAKE)

These are flaky little rolls covered with honey and nuts. They make a great breakfast treat.

1½ cups Primary Batter "B"
4 eggs
½ cup sugar
¾ cup butter
1 tsp salt
3½-4 cups flour
additional butter for brushing
honey and chopped nuts for glaze

Yield: about 24 snail shaped rolls 3-4 inches in diameter.

1. Prepare the Primary Batter "B" following the directions in Chapter 4. Be sure that you have returned 1 cup of the batter to your sourdough starter container before proceeding with the recipe.

2. Assemble all ingredients and utensils. Let all ingredients come to room temperature.

3. Place the 1½ cups of Primary Batter in a warm bowl. Stir in the 4 eggs, the ½ cup of sugar, and the ¾ cup of butter.

4. Stir in the 1 tsp of salt and as much of the flour as possible. When too thick to stir turn the dough out onto a floured board and knead until smooth and satiny.

5. Place in a warm greased bowl, cover and set in a warm place for proofing. The proofing is over when the dough has doubled in size. This should take approximately two hours.

6. Turn the dough out onto a floured board and roll it out very thin. Brush the top of the dough heavily with butter. Fold the dough in half and roll it out thin again. Brush again with butter. Fold it over and roll it out to a thickness of about ½ inch.

7. Cut the dough into strips and using an unfloured portion of the board, shape these strips into ropes by rolling. Twist each rope and then shape the twisted rope into a snail shape. Fold the end under the roll.

8. Place these on a buttered cookie sheet and let rise until doubled in bulk. This will take about 1 hour.

9. Brush the tops with honey and sprinkle heavily with chopped nuts.

10. Bake in a preheated 400 degree oven for 25 minutes. When done, place on a wire rack to cool.

Note: These may be placed in the refrigerator after shaping and kept up to 24 hours before baking. Remove from the refrigerator and set the sheet in a warm 85 degree place for 1½ hours before baking. This will allow you to make them up the night before and serve them hot with breakfast or brunch.

SOURDOUGH LIMPA
(SOURDOUGH SWEDISH RYE)

For a soft, moist rye bread this recipe can't be beaten.

    1½ cups Primary Batter "B"
    1 cup warm milk
    ½ cup brown sugar
    1½ tsp salt
    3 TBS melted butter
    2 tsp caraway seed
    1 tsp fennel seed
    2 TBS grated orange peel
    2 cups rye flour
    2-2¼ cups white flour
Yield. 2 round loaves.

1. Prepare the Primary Batter "B" following the directions in Chapter 4. Before continuing with the recipe be sure that you have returned 1 cup of the batter to your sourdough starter container.

2. Assemble all ingredients and utensils. Let all ingredients come to room temperature.

3. In a large bowl mix together the 1 cup of warm milk, ½ cup of brown sugar, 1½ tsp of salt, 3 TBS melted butter, 2 tsp caraway seed, 1 tsp fennel seed, and 2 TBS of grated orange peel.

4. Stir in the 1½ cups of Primary Batter "B" Add 1 cup of the rye flour and beat vigorously until the batter is smooth. Add the remaining cup of rye flour and stir well.

5. Add 1 cup of the white flour, ½ cup at a time, and beat until the batter is smooth and the flours have been well blended. Add enough more flour (about ½ cup) to make the batter leave the sides of the bowl when stirring.

6. Turn the dough out onto a floured board and knead for about 10 minutes. When the dough is smooth and satiny the kneading is done.

7. Place in a greased bowl, turn over and cover. Place the bowl in a warm spot at 85 degrees for proofing. When the dough has doubled in bulk, about 2 hours later, turn it out and shape into two round loaves.

8. Place the loaves on a greased cookie sheet. Lightly oil the top of the dough and cover it. Set it in a warm 85 degree spot for 1 hour or until doubled in bulk again.

9. Bake in a preheated 350 degree oven until done. Bake on a lower rack. Baking time should be about 45 to 50 minutes. The bread is done when it sounds hollow when thumped. Remove from oven and brush tops with melted butter. Place on wire racks to cool.

SOURDOUGH KULICH
(SOURDOUGH RUSSIAN EASTER BREAD)

This cake-like bread will win all sorts of admiration from your friends.

> 1½ cups Primary Batter "B"
> ¼ cup sugar
> 1 tsp salt
> 2 TBS shortening
> 1 egg
> ¼ cup chopped raisins
> ¼ cup chopped almonds
> 1 tsp grated lemon peel
> 2½ cups flour

Yield: 2 very unique loaves.

1. Prepare the Primary Batter "B" following the directions in Chapter 4. Before proceeding with the recipe, be sure that you have returned one cup of the batter to your sourdough starter container.

2. Assemble all ingredients and utensils. Let all ingredients come to room temperature.

3. Place the 1½ cups of Primary Batter "B" in a warm bowl. Stir in the ¼ cup of sugar, the 1 tsp of salt, and the 2 TBS of melted shortening.

4. Stir in the 1 egg, the ¼ cup chopped raisins, the ¼ cup chopped almonds, and the 1 tsp of grated lemon peel. Beat the mixture vigorously for about a minute.

5. Add enough flour (about 2 cups) to give you a very soft dough. Turn this out onto a floured board and knead in enough additional flour (about ½ cup) to bring the dough to a smooth and elastic consistency.

6. Place the dough in a warm greased bowl and turn the dough over. Cover the bowl and place it in a warm spot for proofing. Let the dough proof until it doubles in bulk. This will take about 2 hours.

7. Punch the dough down. Turn it out onto a well floured board, divide it in two and let it rest for 15 minutes.

8. Place each half in a No. 2 can (normally holds about 1 pound, 4 ounces). Cover and let rise until doubled in bulk. This will take about 1½ hours.

9. Bake in a preheated 350 degree oven for 35-40 minutes or until well browned.

10. Remove from cans at once and cool on wire racks. Spread your favorite white frosting on the top when cool.

SOURDOUGH ENGLISH CURRANT BREAD
(NO-KNEAD)

This is a great tea bread when toasted. It also serves well as a breakfast toast.

      1½ cups Primary Batter "B"
      1 cup warm milk
      1 cup butter
      1 cup sugar
      1 tsp salt
      2 eggs
      1½ cups currants
      ½ tsp mace
      ½ tsp cinnamon
      5-5½ cups flour

Yield: 2 loaves.

1. Prepare the Primary Batter "B" following the directions in Chapter 4. Before adding other ingredients be sure that you have returned 1 cup of the batter to your sourdough starter container.

2. Assemble all ingredients and utensils. Let all ingredients come to room temperature.

3. Heat the 1 cup of milk and the 1 cup of butter and then let cool to lukewarm.

4. Put the 1½ cups of Primary Batter "B" in bowl. Add the milk-butter mixture. Stir in the 1 cup of sugar sifted with the mace and cinnamon added.

5. Stir in the 1 tsp of salt, and the 2 eggs, and the 1½ cups of currants.

6. Stir in the 5-5½ cups of flour. Beat well until smooth. Cover and set in a warm 85 degree place for 2 hours or until doubled in bulk.

7. When doubled, stir down and put into two greased loaf pans. Cover the pans, put them in a warm 85 degree place to rise. When doubled in bulk in approximately 1 hour place in a preheated 400 degree oven.

8. Bake for 15 minutes at 400 degrees, then reduce the heat to 325 degrees and bake an additional 45-55 minutes or until the loaves are browned and done.

9. When done, remove the loaves from the pans and place on wire racks to cool. Brush the tops with melted butter.

Note: Many people prefer raisins to currants. If this is your desire just substitute raisins for currants and you will come out with a delicious loaf.

SOURDOUGH PANETTONE
(SOURDOUGH ITALIAN CHRISTMAS BREAD)

1½ cups Primary Batter "B"
½ cup milk
½ cup sugar
½ cup butter
2 eggs
1 tsp salt
½ cup raisins
½ cup citron
1 TBS anise seed
3½-4 cups flour

Yield: 2 round loaves.

1. Prepare the Primary Batter "B" following the directions in Chapter 4. Be sure that you have returned 1 cup of the batter to your sourdough starter container before proceeding with the recipe.

2. Assemble all ingredients and utensils. Let all ingredients come to room temperature.

3. Put the 1½ cups of Primary Batter "B" in a warm bowl. Add the ½ cup of milk and the ½ cup of sugar.

4. Melt the ½ cup of butter and stir it into the batter.

5. Stir in the 2 eggs, 1 tsp of salt, ½ cup of raisins, ½ cup of citron, 1 TBS of anise seed and enough flour (about 3½ cups) to make the dough leave the sides of the bowl.

6. Turn the dough out onto a floured board and knead in enough additional flour (about ½ cup) until the dough is smooth and blistered. The rough look is due to the raisins and citron.

7. Place the dough in a greased bowl, turn it over and cover. Set the bowl in a warm 85 degree spot for proofing. When doubled in bulk (after about 2 hours) punch the dough down and return it to the same warm place. Let proof until doubled in bulk again (about 45 minutes to 1 hour).

8. Divide the dough into two pieces and form each piece into a round ball. Place on opposite corners of a greased cookie sheet. With a sharp knife, cut to a depth of about ½ inch across the top.

9. Set in a warm 85 degree place until doubled in bulk. This will take about 1 hour. Brush the tops with a mixture of 1 egg with 1 TBS of water.

10. Bake in a preheated 350 degree oven for 45 minutes and then reduce the temperature to 300 degrees and bake for another 15 minutes. The bread is done when the top is browned and sounds hollow when thumped.

11. When done, remove from oven and cool on wire racks.

Note. For a softer crust, brush the top with melted butter just after removing from the oven.

SOURDOUGH KOLACHES

This recipe makes one of the most delicious treats one could ask for. These little fruit topped rolls will make anyone's morning bright.

1½ cups Primary Batter "B"
¾ cup butter or margarine
½ cup sugar
1 tsp salt
4 egg yolks or 2 whole eggs
¼ cup cream or evaporated milk
3-3½ cups flour
12 pitted cooked sweetened prunes

Yield: 12 breakfast rolls.

1. Prepare the Primary Batter "B" following the directions in Chapter 4. Be sure that you have returned 1 cup of the batter to your sourdough starter container before proceeding with your baking.

2. Assemble all ingredients and utensils. Let all ingredients come to room temperature.

3. Cream the ¾ cup of butter with the ½ cup of sugar using the back of a spoon. Add the 1 tsp salt and the 4 egg yolks (or 2 whole eggs) and the ¼ cup of cream (or evaporated milk). Beat with an electric mixer until light and fluffy.

4. Add the 1½ cups of Primary Batter "B" and 1½ cups of flour. Beat well with a wooden spoon scraping down the sides of the bowl often. The batter should be smooth.

5. Stir in enough flour, ½ cup at a time, to make a stiff dough which leaves the sides of the bowl. This will take about 1¾ cups of flour.

6. Place the dough in a greased bowl, turn it over and cover. Set in a warm 85 degree spot until double in bulk. This will take 1-1½ hours.

7. Stir down and turn onto a lightly floured board. Divide into 12 equal pieces and shape each piece into a ball. Cover and let rest for 10 minutes.

8. Place 2 inches apart on greased baking sheets. Press thumb into the center of each ball to make a hollow. There should be about ½-¾ inch rim around the top.

9. Place 1 pitted cooked sweetened prune in hollow. Cover and let rise 30-40 minutes or until doubled in bulk.

10. Bake in a preheated 350 degree oven for 35-40 minutes or until golden brown.

11. After removing from the oven brush the tops with melted butter and sprinkle with powdered sugar or cover with a powdered sugar frosting.

12. Remove from baking sheets and place on a wire rack to cool.

Note: For a variety, use a date filling, apricot filling or any jam that you have around the house. In fact, use several to provide a choice.

SOURDOUGH SOPAIPILLAS

This recipe is an adaptation of the favorite accompaniment to Mexican food in the Albuquerque area. These puffs are served right from the stove. Just bite off a corner and then pour honey into the remainder for a delicious treat.

> 1½ cups Primary Batter "B"
> 4 cups flour
> ½ tsp baking soda
> ½ tsp salt
> 2 TBS shortening
> 1 cup warm milk

Yield: about 36 puffs

1. Prepare the Primary Batter "B" following the directions in Chapter 4. Be sure that you have returned 1 cup of the batter to your storage container before adding any ingredients.

2. Assemble all ingredients and utensils. Let all ingredients come to room temperature.

3. In a 2-quart bowl stir together the 4 cups of flour, ½ tsp baking soda and ½ tsp salt. Cut in the 2 TBS shortening.

4. Add the 1 cup of warm milk to the 1½ cups of Primary Batter "B".

5. Make a well in the center of the dry ingredients and pour the batter-milk mixture into it. Stir well to make a firm dough.

6. Knead the dough 15 to 20 times and set in a warm 85 degree place to rest for 15 minutes.

7. Roll the dough out to 1/8 inch thickness and cut into about 2 inch squares or triangles. Cover the dough.

8. Fry the dough squares in a very hot 420 degree deep fat. The temperature is very important to cause the dough to puff properly. Use a candy thermometer to determine the correct temperature. Fry only a few at a time.

9. Drain on absorbent paper and serve immediately.

Chapter 11
Sourdough Entrees

Your sourdough adventure enters a new and unexplored area with this chapter. For the first time recipes are presented which use your sourdough starter in the actual main dish part of a meal. You will find these recipes are an exciting and unusual addition to your repertory.

SOURDOUGH VEAL BATTER PIE

This quick main course is sure to draw raves. Serve with spinach, broccoli, or green beans.

     1 cup Room Temperature Sourdough Starter
     1 egg beaten
     ⅓ cup flour
     1 tsp salt
     ¼ tsp caraway seed
     1 tsp marjoram
     2 cups cooked veal cubed
     2 TBS butter
Yield: 4 servings.

1. Prepare the Room Temperature Sourdough Starter following the directions in Chapter 4. Be sure to replenish your original starter before proceeding with the recipe.

2. Assemble all ingredients and utensils. Let all ingredients come to room temperature.

3. Add the beaten egg to the 1 cup of sourdough starter. Stir in the ⅓ cup of white flour, 1 tsp salt, ¼ tsp caraway seed and 1 tsp marjoram. Stir well and set in a warm 85 degree spot for 30 minutes.

4. Brown the veal in 2 TBS of butter in a frying pan. Set aside to cool for 20 minutes. Cut the veal into small cubes.

5. Butter a 8½ x 4 loaf pan. Spread the veal out on the bottom of the pan.

6. Add enough warm water to the butter and juices in the frying pan to bring it up to ⅓ cup. Stir this into the batter.

7. Pour the batter over the veal. Bake in a preheated 350 degree oven for 1 hour.

SOURDOUGH MEATLOAF

This meatloaf is tender and juicy with the additional flavoring of sourdough.

> 1 cup Sourdough Starter
> 2 lbs ground beef (lean)
> 1 cup rolled oats or oatmeal
> 1 TBS instant minced onion
> ½ cup warm milk
> 1 egg beaten
> 1 8 oz. can tomato sauce
> 1½ tsp salt
> ¼ tsp black pepper
> 1 tsp Worcestershire Sauce
> 2 TBS brown sugar

Yield: 1 large meat loaf

1. Assemble all ingredients and utensils.

2. Place the rolled oats and instant minced onion in a bowl. Add the ½ cup of warm milk. Let rest for 30 minutes.

3. Beat the egg and add it to the oat mixture.

4. Add the 8 ounces of tomato sauce, 1½ tsp of salt, ¼ tsp of black pepper, 1 tsp of Worcestershire Sauce and the 2 TBS of brown sugar. Blend well making sure that no lumps of rolled oats remain.

5. Remove your sourdough starter from the refrigerator. Take out 1 cup of starter and add it to the oatmeal mixture.

6. Add equal parts of white flour and warm water to your starter to bring it back to its original level in its storage container. Stir well and return to your refrigerator.

7. Place the ground beef in a large bowl and pour the oatmeal starter mixture over it. Work it into the meat until no lumps of meat remain.

8. Place in a large loaf pan (9x5x3 inch) which has been well greased.

9. Bake in a 350 degree oven for 1 hour 15 minutes.

10. After removing from oven let the meat loaf rest for 10 minutes in the serving dish before eating.

SOURDOUGH COUNTRY FRIED CHICKEN

The sourdough batter in which the chicken is dipped before frying imparts a delicious something extra to it.

1 cup Sourdough Starter
¼ cup milk
1 egg beaten
½ tsp poultry seasoning
¼ tsp black pepper
1 tsp salt
¼ tsp baking soda
1 2 to 2½ pound fryer
Yield: 6-8 pieces fried chicken.

1 Remove your sourdough starter from the refrigerator and measure out 1 cup of starter.

2. Add enough white flour and warm water in equal parts to bring the level of starter remaining in your storage container back to its original level. Stir well and return to the refrigerator.

3. Beat the egg and add the ¼ cup of milk. Stir to blend. Add the ½ tsp poultry seasoning, ¼ tsp black pepper and 1 tsp salt. Stir well.

4. Add the ¼ tsp baking soda to the 1 cup of starter and stir well with a wooden or plastic spoon. Add the egg mixture to the starter and stir well.

5. Cut up the fryer, wash well all the pieces and drain them.

6. Dip each piece in batter mix and drop in a frying pan with hot grease or oil about ½ inch thick.

7. Brown well on each side and then lower the heat to simmer and cook for 30 to 45 minutes. Turn once during this period.

8. The chicken is done when the fluid which comes out when pricked with fork is clear rather than cloudy or bloody.

9. Drain and serve with Sourdough Buttermilk Biscuits.

SOURDOUGH PORK CHOP AND RICE CASSEROLE

½ cup sourdough starter
3 cups cooked rice
2 TBS shortening
3 or 4 pork chops
¾ cup milk
½ tsp Worcestershire sauce
½ tsp salt
¼ tsp black pepper
¼ tsp oregano
Yield: Serves 2 or 3

1. Remove your sourdough starter from the refrigerator and measure out ½ cup.

2. To the remaining starter add enough white flour and warm water in equal parts to return the level of the starter to its original height. Stir well and return to the refrigerator.

3. Cook 1 cup of rice until not quite cooked. This will make 3 cups of cooked rice.

4. Melt 2 TBS shortening in a skillet and heat. Brown the 3 or 4 pork chops on both sides.

5. Arrange rice in a 9x11x2 baking pan. Place the browned pork chops on top of the rice.

6. Place the 2 TBS of fat remaining in the skillet and the ¾ cup of milk in a 1-quart bowl. Stir well.

7. Add the ½ tsp Worcestershire sauce, ½ tsp salt, ¼ tsp black pepper and ¼ tsp oregano. Stir well.

8. Add the ½ cup of sourdough starter and stir.

9. Pour this batter over the pork chops and rice.

10. Bake in a preheated 375 oven for 20 minutes.

SOURDOUGH TURKEY CROQUETTES

The surprises called turkey croquettes are given an extra seasoning when made with sourdough.

½ cup sourdough starter
3 TBS melted butter
⅓ cup instant nonfat dry milk
2 egg yolks
2 cups minced cooked turkey
½ tsp dill
1 tsp tarragon
1 tsp salt
1 cup white flour
2 eggs
2 TBS milk
1 TBS oil
1⅓ cups dry bread crumbs

Yield: About 12 croquettes

1. Remove your sourdough starter from the refrigerator and measure out ½ cup of starter.

2. Add enough warm water and white flour in equal parts to the remaining starter to restore it to its original level in the storage container. Stir well and return to the refrigerator.

3. Place the ½ cup of starter, 3 TBS of butter and ⅓ cup of instant non-fat dry milk in a small saucepan and heat until warm but not yet boiling.

4. Beat 2 egg yolks and stir them into the starter mixture. They will cause the batter to thicken slightly.

5. Grease a loaf pan. Add the 2 cups of minced turkey, ½ tsp dill, 1 tsp tarragon, and 1 tsp salt to the batter. Pour it into the pan and set the pan in the refrigerator for 1 hour.

6. Prepare three bowls as follows. In the first place about 1 cup of white flour. In the second stir together about 10-12 times 2 eggs, 2 TBS milk and 1 TBS oil. In the third place 1⅓ cups dry bread crumbs.

7. When the batter is chilled form it into balls about 1 or 1½ inch in diameter. Do not make them larger than 2 inches as they will not cook properly.

8. Dip each ball in the flour, shake off any excess flour then dip it in the egg mixture and finally in the bread crumbs. Shake off gently any excess crumbs. Set the balls on a tray in a warm spot for 20 minutes.

9. Fry in deep fat for 2-4 minutes or until golden brown. The proper temperature for the fat is 385 degrees.

10. Drain and serve immediately.

Note: To reheat use a 400 degree oven.

SOURDOUGH HAMBURGER PIE

Instead of prepackaged meals using ground beef try this one. The hamburger is browned and then baked inside a crust of sourdough.

1 cup sourdough starter
2 eggs beaten
2 TBS melted butter
1 tsp salt
2-2½ cups white flour
1 lb ground beef
4 slices bacon
½ tsp thyme
½ tsp basil
1 egg

Yield: 3 servings.

1. Remove your sourdough starter from the refrigerator and measure out 1 cup of the starter.

2. Add enough warm water and white flour to the remaining starter to bring it up to its original level in its storage container. Stir well and return to refrigerator.

3. Put the 1cup of sourdough starter, 2 beaten eggs, 2 TBS melted butter and 1tsp salt in a 2-quart or larger bowl. Stir well.

4. Add 2 cups of flour, ½ cup at a time. When the dough begins to be soft and sticky turn it out onto a floured bread board and knead gently 8 to 10 times.

5. Place the dough in a greased bowl, turn it over, cover and set in a warm 85 degree spot for 30 minutes to proof.

6. Brown the ground beef in a fry pan. The beef should be lean to prevent excessive shrinkage during baking in the crust. Drain the ground beef and allow to cool for 15 minutes.

7. Stir 4 slices of bacon which have been fried well and then crumbled finely into the ground beef.

8. Stir in the ½ tsp thyme, ½ tsp basil and 1egg.

9. Divide dough and roll or pat each piece into a 9 inch circle. Place the meat mixture on one piece. Put the other piece on top and pinch the edges together.

10. Place the dough filled with beef seam side down in a greased pie pan. Cut a small hole in the top and then place in a preheated 400 degree oven for 30 minutes.

11. Cut into pie shaped wedges to serve. A tomato-cheese sauce goes well with this.

Note: As a variation use half ground beef and half ground pork or half ground lamb. These will provide a variation which will entice your family.

SOURDOUGH TUNA CASSEROLE

Here is a way to give spice to your tuna casserole.

½ cup Room Temperature Sourdough Starter
3 cups large shell macaroni (or 2 cups elbow macaroni)
1 can cream of chicken soup
1 tsp instant minced onion
½ tsp Worcestershire sauce
¼ tsp thyme
¼ tsp salt
1/8 tsp ground black pepper
1 7 oz. can tuna
¼ cup cracker crumbs
shredded cheddar cheese
Yield: 4 servings

1. Prepare the Room Temperature Sourdough Starter following the directions in Chapter 4. Be sure to replenish your original starter before proceeding with the recipe.

2. Assemble all ingredients and utensils. Let all ingredients come to room temperature.

3. Cook the macaroni in salted boiling water according to the directions on the package. Remove from water and drain before done. The macaroni should have firmness to it rather than being completely cooked.

4. Drain well and place in a large bowl.

5. In a separate bowl mix together 1 can cream of chicken soup, 1 tsp instant minced onion, ½ tsp Worcestershire sauce, ¼ tsp thyme, ¼ tsp salt, 1/8 tsp ground black pepper, and the ½ cup of sourdough starter.

6. Add to the macaroni one 7 ounce can of tuna which has been broken up. Stir the soup-starter mixture into the macaroni-tuna mixture. Stir until everything is evenly distributed.

7. Put the mixture in a 2-quart casserole. Sprinkle with cracker crumbs and grated cheddar cheese.

8. Bake in a preheated 350 degree oven for 30 minutes.

9. While the casserole is baking it is time to replace the amount of starter which you removed from its storage container. Add equal parts of white flour and warm water to the remaining starter in amounts sufficient to bring it up to its original level. Stir well and return your starter to the refrigerator.

SOURDOUGH CHICKEN POT PIE

Here is a good way of using that chicken or turkey leftover from a holiday meal.

>¾ cup sourdough starter
>1¾ cup white flour
>½ tsp salt
>½ cup shortening
>2 cups diced chicken (or turkey)
>2 cups broth or stock
>½ cup cooked diced carrots
>½ cup peas
>1/8 tsp celery salt
>¼ tsp salt
>1/8 tsp black pepper
>½ tsp instant onion
>2 TBS flour
>3 TBS water

Yield: Serves 6 (when served with a full dinner), 4 as a main dish

1. Remove your sourdough starter from the refrigerator and measure out ¾ cup of the starter. Set this aside.

2. To the remaining starter add enough warm water and white flour in equal parts to return the level of the starter to its original height. Stir well and return to the refrigerator.

3. Add ½ tsp salt to 1¾ cup of white flour. Cut in ½ cup of shortening until the mixture resembles coarse cornmeal.

4. Add ¾ cup starter and work this into the dough until it forms a ball. Divide the dough into two pieces - one twice the size of the other.

5. Roll the larger of the two pieces out into a large oval. Place this in a oval 1½-quart casserole dish.

6. Prepare the filling as follows. Cook the ½ cup of carrots (in the stock if you wish).

7. Add chicken (or turkey) to the stock and simmer for 10 minutes. Add the carrots, ½ cup peas, 1/8 tsp celery salt, ¼ tsp salt, 1/8 tsp black pepper, ½ tsp instant onion. Stir until well mixed. Bring to boil.

8. Mix together 2 TBS white flour and 3 TBS water. Add this to the filling and stir constantly to thicken. Pour the filling onto the crust in the oval baking dish.

9. Roll the smaller piece of dough into an oval and place on top of the dish. Pinch with the tines of a fork around the edges to seal the bottom crust to the top.

10. Cut several small vent holes in the top crust.

11. Bake in a preheated 375 degree oven until golden brown. This will take about 45 minutes.

SOURDOUGH NOODLES

1 cup Room Temperature Sourdough Starter
2 eggs well beaten
¼ tsp baking soda
¾ tsp salt
2 TBS melted butter
2-3 cups white flour
Yield: 4 servings.

1. Prepare the Room Temperature Sourdough Starter following the directions in Chapter 4. Be sure to replenish your original starter before proceeding with the recipe.

2. Assemble all ingredients and utensils. Let all ingredients come to room temperature.

3. Place the 1 cup of sourdough starter in a warm 1-quart or larger bowl. Add the 2 well beaten eggs.

4. Add the ¼ tsp of baking soda, ¾ tsp salt and the 2 TBS melted butter. Stir well.

5. Add the 2 cups of white flour, ½ cup at a time, stirring well until the dough is stiff and forms a ball that leaves the sides of the bowl.

6. Turn out onto a well floured (1 cup) bread board and divide in half.

7. Roll each half out very, very thin being very sure to keep the dough well floured while rolling.

8. Cut into long strips ½ inch wide. Then cut these strips into 1½ to 2 inch lengths.

9. Flour well and spread out in a flat pan or cookie sheet.

10. Put the noodles into boiling chicken broth or beef broth and cook covered until tender. This is about 15 minutes.

SOURDOUGH ONION RINGS

This delicious recipe comes from Jim and Jeannie Beebe of Manhattan Beach, California. The batter is also great when used with shrimp.

> 1½ cups Primary Batter "B"
> 1 tsp salt
> 1 egg
> ½ cup white flour
> 1 large onion
> oil for frying

Yield: 4 servings.

1. Prepare the Primary Batter "B" following the directions in Chapter 4. Before proceeding with the recipe be sure that you have returned one cup of the batter to your sourdough storage container.

2. Assemble all ingredients and utensils.

3. Put the 1½ cups of Primary Batter "B" in a warm bowl. Add the 1 tsp salt, 1 egg and ½ cup of white flour. Beat with a fork or whisk until the batter is fairly smooth. The batter should be thicker than for pancakes in order for it to cling properly to the onions. If the batter is too thin add a little more flour and if too thick add a bit of water and beat well.

4. Set the batter in a warm spot for 20 minutes while preparing the onion.

5. Peel and slice the onion into approximately ½ inch slices. Separate the slices into rings.

6. Heat the oil in your deep fryer or in your frying pan to a temperature of 380 degrees.

7. Dip the onion rings in the batter to coat them well and fry them two minutes on each side, or until golden brown. Drain on absorbent towels, sprinkle with salt and serve at once.

Chapter 12
Sourdough Cookies

SOURDOUGH DATE FILLED COOKIES

1 cup Room Temperature Sourdough Starter
1 cup sugar
½ cup butter
1 egg
1 tsp vanilla
½ tsp allspice
⅓ cup white flour
2 cups chopped dates

Yield. About 25 date bars.

1 . Prepare the Room Temperature Sourdough Starter following the directions in Chapter 4. Be sure to replenish your original starter before proceeding with the recipe.

2. Assemble all ingredients and utensils. Let all ingredients come to room temperature.

3. Cream 1 cup sugar and ½ cup butter together.

4. Beat the egg.   Stir 1 tsp vanilla and ½ tsp allspice into the butter-sugar .

5. Stir the 1 cup of sourdough starter into the batter, followed by ⅓ cup white flour. Stir well and set in a warm 85 degree spot for 30 minutes.

6. Grease and flour a 9x13 pan and pour half of the batter into the bottom of it. Using a spatula spread it out evenly. Sprinkle the 2 cups of chopped dates evenly over the batter and then pour the remainder of the batter over the top.

7. Bake in a preheated 375 degree oven for 20 minutes or until a toothpick stuck in the batter comes out clean.

8. When cool cut into bars and serve.

SOURDOUGH OATMEAL COOKIES

1½ cups Primary Batter "B"
    (or Room Temperature Sourdough Starter)
1 cup shortening
1 cup white sugar
¼ cup brown sugar
1 egg
¼ cup cream or evaporated milk
1 tsp vanilla
2½ cups flour
½ tsp baking soda
1 tsp salt
1 tsp ground cinnamon
3 cups rolled oats
Yield: 4 dozen 3-inch cookies.

1. Prepare the 1½ cups of Primary Batter "B" or Room Temperature Sourdough Starter following the directions in Chapter 4.

2. Assemble all ingredients and utensils. Let all ingredients come to room temperature.

3. Cream the 1 cup shortening with the 1 cup white sugar and the ¼ cup brown sugar. Beat the egg and stir it in. Add the ¼ cup of cream or evaporated milk and beat until light and fluffy.

4. Stir in the 1½ cups of Primary Batter "B" and the 1 tsp vanilla and mix well.

5. Add the ½ tsp baking soda, the 1 tsp salt and the 1 tsp ground cinnamon to the 2½ cups of white flour and mix well. Add this to the batter, ½ cup at a time, stirring after each addition.

6. Add the 3 cups of rolled oats ½ cup at a time and mix well.

7. Drop by the spoonful onto a greased baking sheet.

8. Bake in a preheated 400 degree oven for 12-15 minutes. When done cool on a wire rack.

Note: 1 cup of raisins or ½ cup of chopped nuts may be added with the rolled oats. Each makes a delicious addition to these cookies.

SOURDOUGH DROP CRUNCHY COOKIES

1½ cups Primary Batter "B"
         (or Room Temperature Sourdough Starter)
½ cup flour
1 cup butter
1¼ cups brown sugar
1 egg
½ tsp salt
½ tsp baking soda
3 cups crushed cornflakes
¾ cup chopped nuts
Yield: about 5 dozen cookies.

1. Prepare the Primary Batter "B" Room Temperature Sourdough Starter following the directions in Chapter 4.

2. Assemble all ingredients and utensils. Let all ingredients come to room temperature.

3. Put the 1½ cups of Primary Batter "B" in a warm bowl. Stir in the ½ cup of flour.

4. In a separate bowl, cream the 1 cup of butter and the 1¼ cups of brown sugar using the back of a spoon.

5. Beat the egg and stir it into the sugar-butter mixture. Stir in the ½ tsp of salt and the ½ tsp of baking soda. Stir in the 3 cups of crushed cornflakes and the ¾ cup of chopped nuts.

6. Stir the two mixtures together.

7. Using a spoon drop the batter onto a greased cookie sheet about two inches apart.

8. Bake in a preheated 375 degree oven for 12-15 minutes. Cool on a wire rack.

SOURDOUGH MOLASSES SQUARES

1 cup Room Temperature Sourdough Starter
¼ cup brown sugar
½ cup butter
1 egg
¾ cup unsulphured molasses
½ tsp salt
1 tsp vanilla
½ tsp cinnamon
¼ tsp baking soda
1⅓ cups flour
Yield: 20 molasses squares.

1. Prepare the Room Temperature Sourdough Starter following the directions in Chapter 4. Be sure to replenish your original starter before proceeding with the recipe.

2. Assemble all ingredients and utensils. Let all ingredients come to room temperature.

3. Beat the egg and add it and the 1 cup of sourdough starter to the butter and brown sugar. Add ¾ cup unsulphured molasses and stir well.

4. Add the ½ tsp salt, 1 tsp vanilla, ½ tsp cinnamon and ¼ tsp baking soda followed by 1⅓ cups flour. Beat the batter for 5 minutes until it is very smooth.

5. Bake in a greased 9x9x2 inch pan in a preheated 375 degree oven for 25 to 30 minutes. The baking is finished when a toothpick stuck into the batter comes out clean.

6. Cut into squares while still warm. Dip the squares in powdered sugar.

SOURDOUGH PEANUT BUTTER DROP COOKIES

1 cup Room Temperature Sourdough Starter
½ cup butter - softened, but not melted
½ cup peanut butter
1 egg beaten
1 cup sugar
½ tsp salt
½ tsp baking soda
¾ cup flour
Yield: About 48 cookies.

1. Prepare the Room Temperature Sourdough Starter following the directions in Chapter 4. Be sure to replenish your original starter before proceeding with the recipe.

2. Assemble all ingredients and utensils. Let all ingredients come to room temperature.

3. Cream together ½ cup butter and 1cup sugar with the back of a spoon. Stir in ½ cup of peanut butter.

4. Beat 1 egg and stir it into the creamed mixture. Stir in 1 cup of room temperature sourdough starter.

5. Stir in ½ tsp salt and ½ tsp baking soda followed by ¾ cup white flour.

6. Using a teaspoon drop heaping teaspoons of the batter onto a greased cookie sheet.

7. Bake in a preheated 375 degree oven for 12-15 minutes. Cool on a wire rack.

SOURDOUGH GUMDROP SQUARES

1½ cups Primary Batter "B"
1 cup shortening
2 cups sugar
2 eggs
½ cup milk
1 tsp vanilla
1 cup white flour
½ cup cocoa
1 tsp salt
1 tsp baking soda
1 cup cut up spiced gum drops
¾ cups chopped walnuts

Yield: About 40 squares.

1. Prepare the Primary Batter following the directions in Chapter 4. Be sure that you have returned 1 cup of the batter to your starter before adding other ingredients.

2. Assemble all ingredients and utensils. Let all ingredients come to room temperature.

3. Cream together 1 cup shortening and 2 cups sugar until light and fluffy. Beat 2 eggs and add to the shortening and sugar.

4. Add ½ cup milk to 1½ cups Primary Batter "B" along with 1 tsp vanilla and stir together.

5. Stir the milk-Primary Batter mixture into the sugar-shortening. Stir until thoroughly mixed.

6. Sift together 1 cup white flour, ½ cup cocoa, 1 tsp salt, and 1 tsp baking soda. Add to the batter and beat well. Add 1 cup spiced gum drops and ¾ cup chopped walnuts to the batter. Stir until all is mixed.

7. Pour into a greased and floured 10x14x1 pan and bake in a pre-heated 375 degree oven for 40 minutes or until a toothpick stuck into the batter comes out clean.

8. Cool in the pan on a wire rack. When cool cut into squares.

Note: If desired these may be frosted or sprinkled with powdered sugar.

Chapter 13
Sourdough Cakes

SOURDOUGH CHOCOLATE CAKE

1½ cups Primary Batter "B"
      (or Room Temperature Sourdough Starter)
4 ounces sweet cooking chocolate
½ cup boiling water
1 tsp baking soda
1 cup butter
2 cups sugar
4 eggs separated
1 tsp vanilla
1 cup flour
½ tsp salt
Yield: 1 three-layer cake.

1. Prepare the Primary Batter "B" or Room Temperature Sourdough Starter following the directions in Chapter 4.

2. Assemble all ingredients and utensils. Let all ingredients come to room temperature.

3. Grease 3 eight or nine-inch pans and cut out circles of waxed paper about 1/8 inch smaller than the pan and place in the pans.

4. Preheat the oven to 350 degrees.

5. Put the ½ cup of water and 4 ounces chocolate in a small pan and bring to a boil, stirring constantly. Pour into glass or china bowl and add the 1 tsp of baking soda and stir until blended. Mixture will foam up. Cool to lukewarm.

6. Put the 1 cup of butter and the 2 cups of sugar in a bowl and cream them together, using the back of a wooden spoon. When just creamy, add the egg yolks one at a time, stirring well after each addition.

7. Stir in the 1 tsp of vanilla and the melted chocolate and water

8. Put the 1 cup of flour and the ½ tsp of salt in a small bowl and stir together.

9. Stir ½ cup of the Primary Batter "B" into the butter-sugar-egg yolk mixture. Stir in ½ cup of the flour and then ½ cup more of the Primary Batter "B" , followed by the final ½ cup of the flour and then the final ½ cup of the Primary Batter "B". Be sure to stir well after each addition. Beat the batter until it is smooth.

10. Beat the egg whites until they are stiffly beaten. Fold the stiffly beaten egg whites gently into the batter.

11. Pour the batter into the cake pans ⅔ full and pick each pan up and drop it from the height of 4 inches squarely on a flat surface.

12. Bake in the preheated 350 degree oven for 35 minutes. The cake is done when a toothpick stuck in the center of the pan comes out clean.

13. Remove form oven and let cool for about 5 minutes. Then turn the layers out onto wire racks to cool. Frost when completely cool with your favorite frosting.

SOURDOUGH COCOA CAKE

1½ cups Primary Batter "B"
    (or Room Temperature Sourdough Starter)
½ cup cocoa
1 tsp baking soda
1 cup boiling water
½ cup butter
½ cup shortening
2 cups sugar
3 eggs well beaten
1 tsp vanilla
1 tsp salt
½ cup buttermilk
1 cup flour

Yield: 1 two-layer chocolate cake.

1. Prepare the Primary Batter "B" or Room Temperature Sourdough Starter following the directions in Chapter 4.

2. Assemble all ingredients and utensils. Let all ingredients come to room temperature.

3. Put the ½ cup of cocoa and the 1 tsp baking soda in a bowl. Add the 1 cup of boiling water and stir. It will be foamy. Let set for 20 minutes until cool.

4. Cream together, using the back of a wooden spoon, the ½ cup of butter, ½ cup of shortening and the 2 cups of sugar.

5. Stir the 3 beaten eggs, 1 tsp vanilla and the 1 tsp salt into the sugar-butter mixture. Beat with an electric mixer until light and fluffy.

6. Add the cocoa mixture, blend and beat again until light and fluffy.

7. Using a wooden spoon, add the ½ cup of buttermilk to the 1½ cups of Primary Batter "B". Add this mixture alternately with the flour to the beaten mixture. Do this by adding ⅓ of the batter- buttermilk mixture and then ½ cup of flour, then ⅓ of the batter mixture, then ½ cup of flour, and then the final ⅓ of the batter mixture. Beat well after each addition.

8. Pour the batter into 2 greased and floured 9-inch round cake pans. They should be about ⅔ full.

9. Place in a preheated 350 degree oven and bake for 35 minutes.

10. Remove from the oven when done (a toothpick comes out clean) and let set in the pan for a few minutes. Then turn out onto a wire rack to cool.

11 . When completely cool, frost with your favorite frosting.

SOURDOUGH FRUITCAKE

1½ cups Primary Batter "B"
    (or Room Temperature Sourdough Starter)
1½ cups white raisins
1½ cups currants
1 cup diced candied cherries (red)
½ cup diced candied pineapple (plain or yellow)
½ cup diced candied pineapple (green)
½ cup diced candied orange peel
½ cup diced candied lemon peel
1 cup Sherry (not cooking sherry)
1½ cups granulated sugar
½ cup golden brown sugar
⅔ cup shortening
1½ tsp cinnamon
1 tsp nutmeg
2 eggs well beaten
2 cups chopped pecans
4 cups flour
1 tsp baking soda
2 tsp salt

Yield: 2 loaves of fruit cake.

1. Prepare the Primary Batter "B" or Room Temperature Sourdough Starter following the directions in Chapter 4.

2. Wash the raisins and currants and drain. Chop the raisins. Mix together the chopped raisins, currants, and all the candied fruit. Pour the 1 cup of Sherry over them and stir well. Cover and let set overnight.

3. Assemble all ingredients and utensils. Let all ingredients come to room temperature.

4. Cream the 1½ cups of sugar, the ½ cup of brown sugar and the ⅔ cup shortening with the back of a wooden spoon. Add the spices. Beat in the 2 eggs.

5. Sift the 4 cups of flour, 1 tsp of baking soda, and the 2 tsp of salt together.

6. Stir in the 1½ cups of Primary Batter "B" into the sugar mixture. Stir in the 2 cups pecans and the fruit mixture.

7. Stir the 4 cups of the flour mixture into the batter, ½ cup at a time, stirring after each addition. Stir until no lumps remain.

8. Grease two 9-inch loaf pans. Line them with heavy brown paper and grease this paper. Pour the batter into these pans equally.

9. Bake in a preheated 275 degree oven for 2½ hours.

10. Remove from pans and cool on wire racks. Remove paper after cool.

11. After spooning 2 or 3 spoonfuls of Sherry over the top of each loaf, wrap them in aluminum foil and store in the refrigerator. Periodically open the wrapping and add more Sherry. Let ripen for at least 1 month before serving. May be kept almost indefinitely if kept tightly wrapped between additions of Sherry.

Note: If desired, Brandy may be used in place of Sherry.

SOURDOUGH OATMEAL CAKE

1½ cups Primary Batter "B"
      (or Room Temperature Sourdough Starter)
1 cup boiling water
1 cup rolled oats (or oatmeal)
½ cup butter or shortening
1 cup sugar
1 cup brown sugar
1 tsp vanilla
2 eggs
½ tsp salt
¾ tsp cinnamon
¼ tsp nutmeg
1 cup flour

Yield: 1 9x9 cake.

1. Prepare the Primary Batter "B" or Room Temperature Sourdough Starter following the directions in Chapter 4.

2. Assemble all ingredients and utensils. Let all ingredients come to room temperature.

3. Pour the 1 cup of boiling water over the 1 cup of rolled oats in a bowl, stir and let set for 20 minutes or until lukewarm.

4. Cream the ½ cup of butter, the 1 cup of sugar and the 1 cup of brown sugar together using the back of a spoon. Add the 1 tsp of vanilla and the 2 eggs, one at a time, and beat well.

5. Add the ½ tsp salt, the ¾ tsp cinnamon and the ¼ tsp nutmeg. Add the oatmeal mixture and stir well.

6. Stir in the 1½ cups of Primary Batter "B" and the 1 cup of flour, beating well after adding each.

7. Pour the batter into a greased and floured 9x9x2 inch pan. The pan will be about ¾ full.

8. Bake in a preheated 350 degree oven for 1 hour and 15 minutes. The cake is done when a toothpick stuck in the center comes out clean.

9. Cool in the pan and frost with your favorite light frosting.

SOURDOUGH APPLESAUCE CAKE 1

This tasty cake recipe was sent to us by Mrs. Grace Rowden of Jacksonville, Oregon.

> 1½ cups Primary Batter "B"
>   (or Room Temperature Sourdough Starter)
> ½ cup shortening
> 2 cups sugar
> 2 eggs
> 1½ cups applesauce
> 1 tsp cinnamon
> ½ tsp cloves
> ½ tsp allspice
> 1½ tsp salt
> 1½ tsp baking soda
> 2 TBS sugar
> 2 cups flour
> 1 cup raisins
> ½ cup chopped walnuts

Yield: 1 9x12x2 inch cake.

1. Prepare the Primary Batter "B" or Room Temperature Sourdough Starter following the directions in Chapter 4.

2. Assemble all ingredients and utensils. Let all ingredients come to room temperature.

3. Cream together the ½ cup shortening and the 2 cups of sugar.

4. Beat in the 2 eggs.

5. Stir in the 1½ cups Primary Batter "B", 1½ cups applesauce, 1 tsp cinnamon, ½ tsp cloves and ½ tsp allspice.

6. In a small bowl blend together the 1½ tsp salt 1½ tsp baking soda and the 2 TBS sugar.

7. Sprinkle this over the cake batter and stir in gently.

8. Add 2 cups flour and stir until smooth. Add 1 cup raisins and ½ cup chopped walnuts. Stir well.

9. Pour into greased and floured 9x12x2 pan and bake for 45 minutes at 350 degrees.

10. Alternately pour into two 8x8x1½ inch square pans and bake at 350 degrees for 25 minutes.

11. Let cool in pan(s).

SOURDOUGH APPLESAUCE CAKE II

This delicious applesauce cake recipe comes from Helen C. Cole of San Francisco. It will prove to be one of your favorites as it is ours.

1 cup Room Temperature Sourdough Starter
¼ cup dry skim milk (instant nonfat dry milk)
1 cup applesauce
1 cup white flour
1 cup sugar
½ cup brown sugar
½ cup butter
1 egg beaten
1 tsp salt
1 tsp cinnamon
1 tsp nutmeg
½ tsp allspice
½ tsp ground cloves
2 tsp baking soda
½ cup chopped nuts
(or a combination of chopped nuts and raisins)

Yield: 1 delicious 9x12x2 cake

1. Prepare the Room Temperature Sourdough Starter following the directions in Chapter 4. Be sure to replenish your original starter before proceeding with the recipe.

2. Assemble all ingredients and utensils. Let all ingredients come to room temperature.

3. Place the 1 cup of starter in a warm bowl and add ¼ cup dry skim milk, 1 cup of applesauce and 1 cup white flour. Stir and set in a warm 85 degree place while proceeding with the recipe.

4. Cream together with the back of a spoon 1 cup sugar, ½ cup brown sugar and ½ cup butter.

5. Beat 1 egg and add it to the sugar-butter mixture. Beat well.

6. Add 1 tsp salt, 1 tsp cinnamon, 1 tsp nutmeg, ½ tsp allspice, ½ tsp ground cloves, 2 tsp baking soda and ½ cup chopped nuts (or a combination of chopped nuts and raisins).

7. Combine the creamed mixture with the sourdough mixture and beat by hand for 100 strokes.

8. Pour into a greased and floured 9x12x2 baking dish and put in a preheated 350 degree oven for 30-35 minutes or until a toothpick stuck in the cake comes out clean.

9. When done remove from oven and let cool in pan.

10. Serve with whipped cream or frost with a coconut or mocha frosting.

SOURDOUGH UPSIDEDOWN APPLE CAKE

1½ cups Primary Batter "B"
4 cups sliced cooking apples
½ cup sugar
1 tsp cinnamon
½ cup brown sugar
½ cup milk
¾ tsp salt
1 tsp baking soda
1 cup flour
¼ cup melted shortening (cooled)
1 egg beaten
1 tsp vanilla

Yield: 1 9x12x2 cake

1. Prepare Primary Batter "B" following the directions in Chapter 4. Be sure that you have returned 1 cup of the batter to your sourdough storage container before adding other ingredients.

2. Assemble all ingredients and utensils. Let all ingredients come to room temperature.

3. Peel and slice the apples. Place them in an ungreased 9x12x2 baking pan. Sprinkle ½ cup sugar and 1 tsp of cinnamon over the top. If the apples are extremely tart you may wish to increase the amount of sugar.

4. Place the 1½ cups of Primary Batter "B" in a 2-quart or larger bowl. Stir in ½ cup brown sugar and ½ cup milk at room temperature.

5. Stir in ¾ tsp salt, 1 tsp baking soda and 1 cup of white flour.

6. Add ¼ cup of melted shortening which has been allowed to cool to room temperature. Stir in 1 tsp vanilla. Stir vigorously. You will have a soft batter.

7. Pour the batter over the apples. Place in a preheated 375 degree oven and bake for 30-35 minutes or until a cake tester (or toothpick) comes out clean when inserted into the cake.

8. Serve plain or upside down with whipped cream.

SOURDOUGH GINGERBREAD 1

1½ cups Primary Batter "B"
     (or Room Temperature Sourdough Starter)
½ cup butter or shortening
½ cup sugar
1 egg beaten
1 cup molasses
1 tsp cinnamon
1 tsp ginger
½ tsp salt
¼ tsp baking soda
½ cup flour

Yield: 1 9-inch square gingerbread delight.

1. Prepare the Primary Batter "B" Room Temperature Sourdough Starter following the directions in Chapter 4.

2. Assemble all ingredients and utensils. Let all ingredients come to room temperature.

3. Cream together the ½ cup of butter and the ½ cup of sugar. Add the beaten egg and mix well.

4. Add the 1 cup of molasses and beat well. Add the 1½ cups of Primary Batter "B", 1 tsp of cinnamon, 1 tsp of ginger, ½ tsp of salt, and the ¼ tsp of baking soda to the mixture.

5. Add the ½ cup of flour and beat about 2 minutes. Scrape down the sides and then pour into a greased and floured 9x9x2 inch pan.

6. Bake in a preheated 350 degree oven for 55 minutes. It is done when a toothpick stuck in the center comes out clean.

7. Cool either inside or outside of the pan.

SOURDOUGH GINGERBREAD II

This gingerbread is so moist that you can hear the moisture when you gently squeeze a piece of it. The recipe is from Mrs. Ellen Slutsky of Beverly Hills, California.

1 cup Room Temperature Sourdough Starter
1½ cups milk
2 cups whole wheat flour
1 cup wheat germ (or ½ cup cornmeal and ½ cup other flour)
1⅓ cups dark unsulphered or blackstrap molasses
⅔ cup honey
3 eggs beaten
½ cup oil
1 tsp salt
1 TBS cinnamon
1 TBS ginger
½ tsp nutmeg
½ tsp allspice
1 tsp baking soda
Yield: 1 9x12x2 inch moist gingerbread

1. Prepare the Room Temperature Sourdough Starter following the directions in Chapter 4. Be sure to replenish your original starter before proceeding with the recipe.
2. Assemble all ingredients and utensils. Let all ingredients come to room temperature.
3. Add the 1½ cups of milk to the 1 cup of starter. Stir in 2 cups of whole wheat flour.
4. Add the 1 cup of wheat germ (or substitute) and the 1⅓ cups of molasses. Stir well .
5. Add the ⅔ cups honey, 3 beaten eggs and ½ cup oil. Stir gently.
6. Mix together 1 tsp of salt, 1 TBS cinnamon, 1 TBS ginger, ½ tsp nutmeg, ½ tsp allspice, and 1 tsp baking soda. Sprinkle this over the top of the batter and then stir in gently.
7 . Pour into a greased 9x12x2 inch pan and bake in a preheated 350 degree oven for 40 minutes.
8. Let cool in pan before serving or storing.

SOURDOUGH JAM CAKE

This recipe produces a moist very sweet cake.

1 cup Room Temperature Sourdough Starter
1 cup butter
1 cup sugar
1 cup seedless blackberry jam
(or any other jam)
3 egg whites beaten
1 cup flour
1 tsp cinnamon
1 tsp allspice
1 tsp cloves
1 tsp baking soda
Yield: 1 8 inch two layer cake

1. Prepare the Room Temperature Sourdough Starter following the directions in Chapter 4. Be sure to replenish your original starter before proceeding with the recipe.

2. Assemble all ingredients and utensils. Let all ingredients come to room temperature.

3. Cream the 1 cup of butter. Add the 1 cup of sugar and cream until light.

4. Using a blender or electric mixer add 1 cup of blackberry jam to the butter-sugar mixture.

5. Beat the egg whites until frothy but not yet stiff.

6. Mix together in a dry bowl the 1 cup of flour and all the spices.

7. Put the butter-sugar-jam mixture in a large bowl. Add the 1 cup of sourdough starter and the egg whites. Add the flour mixture beating just enough to blend.

8. Pour into 2 greased 8 inch cake tins and bake in a preheated 350 degree oven for 30 minutes or until a toothpick stuck into the center comes out clean.

9. When done remove from pans and cool on wire rack. After thoroughly cool frost with a white frosting and decorate with more of the jam used in the cake.

SOURDOUGH MYSTERY DESERT

A desert halfway between a pudding and a cake which grows more moist with age.

> 1 cup Room Temperature Sourdough Starter
> 1 cup white flour
> ¾ cup sugar
> 1 tsp baking soda
> ½ tsp salt
> 1 egg
> 1 tsp vanilla
> 1 can (17 oz.) fruit cocktail (drained)
> ¼ cup juice from fruit cocktail
> ½ cup brown sugar
> ½ cup chopped walnuts

Yield: 1 8x8 cake serving 9

1. Prepare the Room Temperature Sourdough Starter following the directions in Chapter 4. Be sure to replenish your original starter before proceeding with the recipe.

2. Assemble all ingredients and utensils. Let all ingredients come to room temperature.

3. In a small bowl stir together 1 cup white flour, ¾ cup sugar, 1 tsp baking soda, and ½ tsp salt.

4. Put the starter in a warm bowl. Add 1 beaten egg, 1 tsp vanilla, 1 can of fruit cocktail which has been drained and ¼ cup of the juice from the draining. Stir well.

5. Add this mixture to the flour and stir only long enough to dampen.

6. Pour into a greased 8x8x1½ pan.

7. Mix together ½ cup brown sugar and ½ cup chopped walnuts. Sprinkle this on top of the batter in the pan.

8. Bake in a preheated 350 degree oven for 45 minutes or until a toothpick inserted into the cake comes out clean.

9. Cool in the pan on a wire rack. Cut into squares or wedges and serve with whipped cream.

SOURDOUGH NUT CAKE

1½ cups Primary Batter "B"
1 cup shortening
2 cups sugar
3 eggs
½ cup milk
1 tsp vanilla
1 cup white flour
½ tsp baking soda
1 cup chopped pecans
Yield: 1 cake

1. Prepare the Primary Batter "B" following the directions in Chapter 4. Be sure that you have returned 1 cup of the batter to your starter storage container before adding other ingredients.

2. Assemble all ingredients and utensils. Let all ingredients come to room temperature.

3. Cream 1 cup shortening and 2 cups sugar together until creamy.

4. Beat 3 eggs until light and fluffy and add them to the shortening-sugar mixture.

5. Stir in 1 tsp vanilla, 1½ cups Primary Batter "B" and ½ cup milk. Stir well.

6. Stir ½ tsp baking soda into 1 cup white flour and then stir the flour into the batter a small amount at a time. Stir in 1 cup chopped nuts.

7. Pour the batter into a round tube pan and bake in a preheated 375 degree oven for 1 hour 10 minutes or until a toothpick stuck into the cake comes out clean.

8. Frost when cool with a favorite frosting.

SOURDOUGH POTATO CAKE

1 cup Room Temperature Sourdough Starter
1 cup sugar
½ cup butter
2 eggs
2 tsp baking soda
¾ tsp salt
½ tsp cinnamon
½ tsp nutmeg
½ tsp ground cloves
1 cup mashed potatoes
½ cup white flour
½ cup chopped nuts
Yield: 1 8x8x2 cake.

1. Prepare the Room Temperature Sourdough Starter following the directions in Chapter 4. Be sure to replenish your original starter before proceeding with the recipe.

2. Assemble all ingredients and utensils. Let all ingredients come to room temperature.

3. Cream together with the back of a spoon 1 cup sugar and ½ cup butter.

4. Beat 2 eggs and stir them into the butter and sugar.

5. Stir in 2 tsp baking soda, ¾ tsp salt, ½ tsp cinnamon ½ tsp nutmeg, ½ tsp ground cloves.

6. Stir in 1 cup of mashed potatoes (room temperature) and ½ cup flour. Stir in ½ cup chopped nuts. Stir until well blended.

7. Pour the batter into a 8x8x2 greased and floured baking pan.

8. Bake in a preheated 350 degree oven for 40-45 minutes or until a toothpick stuck in the cake comes out clean and the top is browned.

9. Cool in pan for 5 minutes then remove from pan and cool on wire rack.

10. Serve either warm or cold. Whipped cream goes well with this cake.

Chapter 14
Sourdough Pie, Puddings
& Other Desserts

SOURDOUGH CINNAMON ROLLS

1½ cups Primary Batter "B"
     (or Room Temperature Sourdough Starter)
¾ cup milk
½ tsp vanilla
2 TBS sugar
1 TBS melted butter
1 tsp salt
2 to 2⅓ cups flour
1 tsp cinnamon
¼ cup sugar
melted butter
Yield. 14 sourdough cinnamon rolls.

1. Prepare the Primary Batter "B" or Room Temperature Sourdough Starter following the directions in Chapter 4.

2. Assemble all ingredients and utensils. Let all ingredients come to room temperature.

3. Place the 1½ cups of Primary Batter "B" or Room Temperature Sourdough Starter in a warm 3-quart or larger bowl.

4. Add the ½ tsp of vanilla, the ¾ cup of milk, 2 TBS sugar, 1 TBS melted butter and 1 tsp salt and stir well.

5. Add 2 cups of flour, ½ cup at a time, until too stiff to stir with a spoon.

6. Turn the dough onto a well floured board and knead in enough additional flour (about ⅓ cup) to make the dough smooth and elastic. This is a soft dough.

7. Place the dough in a greased bowl, turn over, cover the bowl, and place in a warm spot for proofing. In 2 hours when the dough has doubled in bulk, punch it down and turn it out onto a floured board. Roll or pat with your hands the dough until it is in the shape of a rectangle and about ½ inch thick.

8. Brush the dough with melted butter and sprinkle generously with the ¼ cup of sugar and the 1 tsp cinnamon mixed together.

9. Roll up, starting with the short side into a long roll. Cut this roll into 1 inch thick slices and place them in a greased pan with the sides touching and the cross section of the roll upwards. Cover and let rise until doubled in bulk. This will take 45 minutes to an hour.

10. Bake in a preheated 400 degree oven for 25-30 minutes. Remove the pan from the oven and cool in the pan on a wire rack.

11. Drizzle with medium powdered sugar icing (milk, powdered sugar and a drop or two of vanilla) while still warm.

SOURDOUGH RICH CHOCOLATE BROWNIES

1½ cups Primary Batter "B"
      (or Room Temperature Sourdough Starter)
4 ounces sweet cooking chocolate
½ cup hot water
1 tsp baking soda
1 cup butter
2 cups sugar
4 eggs separated
1½ tsp vanilla
1 cup flour
¾ tsp salt

Yield: 1 11x16 pan of brownies.

1. Prepare the Primary Batter "B" or Room Temperature Sourdough Starter following the directions in Chapter 4.

2. Assemble all ingredients and utensils. Let all ingredients come to room temperature.

3. Generously grease and flour a 11x16 inch pan.

4. Preheat your oven to 350 degrees.

5. Put 4 ounces of sweet cooking chocolate in a small pan. Add ½ cup of hot water and bring to a boil. Stir constantly. Pour into a china or glass bowl and add the 1 tsp of baking soda and mix. The mixture will foam. Let it set to cool until lukewarm. This takes about 20 minutes.

6. Put 1 cup of butter and 2 cups sugar in a large bowl. Cream together until fluffy, using the back of a wooden spoon. When creamy, add egg yolks one at a time and stir well after each addition.

7. Stir in the 1½ tsp of vanilla and the cooled chocolate mix.

8. Stir the ¾ tsp of salt into the 1 cup of flour.

9. Stir ½ cup of the Primary Batter "B" into the butter-egg-sugar mixture. Stir in ½ cup of flour-salt and then ½ cup more of the
Primary Batter "B" followed by the final ½ cup of flour and then the final ½ cup of Primary Batter "B" Be sure that you stir vigorously after each addition.

10. Beat the egg whites until they form stiff peaks. Fold the beaten egg whites gently into the batter until well blended.

11. Pour batter into the greased and floured 11 by 16 inch pan and let set for 30 minutes in a warm 85 degree place.

12. Bake in a preheated 350 degree oven for 35-40 minutes. The brownies are done when a toothpick stuck in the center comes out clean.

13. Remove from the oven and let set about 5 minutes. Then invert the pan on a large cooling rack and let the brownies cool.

Note. These brownies are delicious when frosted with a rich chocolate icing.

SOURDOUGH DOUGHNUTS

1½ cups Primary Batter "B"
      (or Room Temperature Sourdough Starter)
1 egg
¼ tsp vanilla
¼ cup milk
2 TBS cooking oil
2 cups flour
¼ tsp baking soda
¼ cup sugar
¾ tsp salt
Yield: 18-20 doughnuts.

1. Prepare the Primary Batter "B" or Room Temperature Sourdough Starter following the directions in Chapter 4.

2. Assemble all ingredients and utensils. Let all ingredients come to room temperature.

3. Place the 1½ cups of Primary Batter "B" in a warm 4-quart bowl.

4. Beat the egg and mix it, the ¼ tsp of vanilla, and the ¼ cup of milk into the batter. Add the 2 TBS of cooking oil.

5. Measure out the 2 cups of flour and sift it with the ¼ tsp baking soda, the ¼ cup of sugar, and the ¾ tsp of salt into the batter. Mix well.

6. Turn the dough out onto a floured board and knead slightly to firm up and round out the dough. The dough is soft but easy to handle.

7. Roll out the dough on the board to ½ inch thickness. Cut with a doughnut cutter and place the doughnuts on a lightly greased and floured sheet. Place the cookie sheet in a warm place at 85 degrees for about 30 minutes to let the doughnuts rise.

8 . Lift the doughnuts gently off the cookie sheet and drop them in hot fat or oil at 400 degrees. This is a higher temperature than non-sourdough doughnuts are cooked at, but is necessary for good doughnuts. Fry for 1½ minutes on each side. They should be golden brown at this time. Fry no more than three at a time, to prevent the temperature of the fat from dropping too low.

9. Drain on absorbent paper and dip in glaze (recipe following) or dust with powdered or granulated sugar.

Glaze

Mix powdered sugar, soft butter, a little vanilla, add a dash of cinnamon with enough warm milk to make a thin batter.

Eat sourdough doughnuts when fresh for the best taste. They can be frozen and when ready to use, heat them at 425 degrees in your oven in a covered pan for 10 minutes to thaw. These doughnuts have a texture somewhere between that of a cake doughnut and of a regular raised doughnut.

SOURDOUGH FLUFFY DOUGHNUTS

These are fluffy, light doughnuts which just melt in your mouth. The recipe is from Larry Pickle of Buena Park, California.

> 1½ cups Primary Batter "B"
> 2 eggs
> ½ tsp vanilla
> ¼ cup milk
> 2 TBS cooking oil
> 2½ cups sifted white flour
> ¼ tsp baking soda
> ½ cup sugar
> ¾ tsp salt
> ½ tsp cinnamon and/or nutmeg

Yield: 24 large doughnuts.

1. Prepare Primary Batter "B" following the directions in Chapter 4. Be sure that you have returned 1 cup of the batter to your sourdough starter container before continuing with the recipe.

2. Assemble all ingredients and utensils. Let all ingredients come to room temperature.

3. Place the 1½ cups of Primary Batter "B" in a warm 4-quart bowl.

4. Beat the eggs and add them with ½ tsp vanilla and the ¼ cup milk to the batter and stir. Add the 2 TBS cooking oil.

5. Measure out 2 cups of white flour and sift it with the ¼ tsp baking soda, ½ cup of sugar, ¾ tsp salt and ½ tsp nutmeg and/or cinnamon into the batter. Mix well.

6. Turn the dough (really a smooth, heavy batter) out onto a floured board and knead in enough additional sifted flour (about ½ cup) to produce a dough that is light but elastic. This is so when a finger gently pressed into the dough (without breaking the surface) and then retracted leaves a depression that quickly springs back.

7. Place the dough in a well greased bowl and place in a 85 degree place for proofing. When the dough is doubled in bulk, about 2 to 2½ hours turn it out onto a lightly floured board.

8. Flour your hands and knead dough only long enough to remove the stickiness from the outside of the dough. At *no* time do you punch down the dough or knead it vigorously. Such actions would cause your doughnuts to be heavy.

9. Roll the dough out into an oval shape about ½ inch thick. Cut doughnuts and place on a floured cookie sheet. Place in a 85 degree spot for 30-45 minutes for proofing.

10. Gently remove raised doughnuts from the cookie sheet and drop into hot oil or fat at 350 degrees. Fry for about 1½ minutes on each side or until golden brown.

11. Drain and glaze or dust with sugar.

Note: This dough at the stage it is in at the beginning of Step 9 is also good for cinnamon rolls, many coffee cakes and baked or fried fruit pies made from sourdough doughs. Be adventurous with yourself.

SOURDOUGH FRIED APPLE PIE

¾ cup Room Temperature Sourdough Starter
½ cup shortening
1 tsp salt
2 cups white flour
Yield: 6 large or 8 medium individual fried apple pies

1. Prepare the Room Temperature Sourdough Starter following the directions in Chapter 4. Be sure to replenish your original starter before proceeding with the recipe.

2. Assemble all ingredients and utensils. Let all ingredients come to room temperature.

3. Sift 2 cups of white flour twice, the second time with 1 tsp salt.

4. Cut ¼ cup of shortening into the dough with a knife or pastry cutter. Next cut the other ¼ cup of shortening in until the dough is pea sized.

5. Stir in ¾ cup of sourdough starter very gently only moistening the flour shortening mixture. Form a dough ball with as little handling as possible.

6. Divide the dough into 6 pieces and roll each piece out to a thickness of about 1/8 inch.

7. On each piece place 1/6 of the filling (recipe below) and then fold the dough over the filling so that you have a half circle. Seal the edge where the crusts meet with the tines of a fork.

8. Place the pies, two at a time, in a skillet containing about ½ inch of hot fat. Cook until brown on each side.

9. Drain on paper towels and sprinkle with sugar. Serve hot.

Filling :

3 cups thinly sliced or diced cooking apples
½ cup sugar
1 tsp cinnamon
1 tsp nutmeg
¼ tsp salt
4 TBS white flour

1. Combine all the ingredients except the apples.

2. Stir the apples into the other ingredients making sure that they are thoroughly coated.

SOURDOUGH APPLE FRITTERS

1 cup Room Temperature Sourdough Starter
1 egg
½ tsp salt
2 TBS brown sugar
¼ tsp cinnamon
¼ tsp nutmeg
¼ cup shortening
¾ cup flour
1 cup diced cooking apples
Yield: About 20 tempting apple fritters

1. Prepare the Room Temperature Sourdough Starter following the directions in Chapter 4. Be sure to replenish your original starter before proceeding with the recipe.

2. Assemble all ingredients and utensils. Let all ingredients come to room temperature.

3. Beat the 1 egg and add it to the 1 cup of sourdough starter.

4. Stir in ½ tsp salt, 2 TBS brown sugar, ¼ tsp cinnamon, ¼ tsp nutmeg and ¼ cup melted shortening. Stir well.

5. Add about ¾ cup of white flour a little at a time. The dough has the right amount of flour when it drips off a spoon in 1½ inch ribbons when held up. Now stir until you have an extremely smooth batter. Add 1 cup of diced cooking apples. The apples should not be mushy or overripe.

6. Cover the batter and set it in a 85 degree spot for 2 hours. This is important to properly break down the gluten in order that the fritters will puff properly.

7. Drop tablespoonfuls of the batter into deep fat at 380 degrees. A candy thermometer can be used to determine the correct temperature. Cook for 2 minutes or until golden brown.

8. Drain and serve immediately. The moisture in the fruit causes any fritters which haven't been eaten to soften when stored. You may reheat in a 400 degree oven for 15 minutes to restore some of the crispness.

SOURDOUGH APPLE BROWN BETTY

2 cups soft sourdough bread crumbs
2 TBS butter
3 cups chopped cooking apples
½ cup sugar
½ tsp cinnamon
1/8 tsp salt
½ tsp nutmeg
¼ cup water
juice of ½ lemon

Yield. 6 servings.

1. Melt 2 TBS butter and stir it into 2 cups of soft sourdough bread crumbs. The bread crumbs may be from any type of sourdough bread. The great variety of sourdough breads will give you a chance to serve a variety of deserts with the same recipe.

2. In a separate bowl place 3 cups of chopped cooking apples. Add ½ cup sugar, ½ tsp cinnamon, 1/8 tsp salt, ½ tsp nutmeg ¼ cup water and the juice of ½ lemon. Stir until thoroughly mixed.

3. Butter a baking dish and place ⅓ of the bread crumbs on the bottom of it. Cover these with ½ of the apples, then ⅓ of the bread crumbs, the final ½ of the apples and then the last ⅓ of the bread crumbs.

4. Bake in a preheated 375 degree oven for 45-60 minutes. Cover the baking dish for the first 20 minutes of baking. The desert is done when the crumbs are brown and the apples are tender.

5. Serve warm with hard sauce.

SOURDOUGH BANANA PUFFS

These make a delightful breakfast treat or a wonderful desert.

> 1½ cups Primary Batter "B"
> 1 TBS sugar
> ½ tsp salt
> 2 TBS butter
> 1 egg beaten
> 1¾ cups white flour
> 3 ripe bananas
> ½ tsp cinnamon
> ½ tsp ginger
> 2 TBS sugar

Yield: About 16 to 18 puffs

1. Prepare the Primary Batter "B" following the directions in Chapter 4. Be sure that you have returned 1 cup of the batter to your sourdough storage container before adding other ingredients.

2. Assemble all ingredients and utensils. Let all ingredients come to room temperature.

3. Put the 1½ cups of Primary Batter "B" in 1-quart or larger bowl. Stir in 1 TBS sugar, ½ tsp salt and 2 TBS of melted butter.

4. Beat the egg and stir it and 1 cup of the flour into the starter.

5. This is a very sticky dough. Turn onto a floured bread board and gently knead in approximately ¾ cup of white flour. Place the dough in a greased bowl, turn it over, cover the bowl, and set it in a warm 85 degree place for 2 hours or until doubled in bulk.

6. Turn the dough out when the proofing is finished and roll it out to a thickness of about ¼ inch. Cut the dough into 3 inch circles.

7. Make a mixture by mashing 3 ripe bananas and adding to them ½ tsp cinnamon, ½ tsp ginger and 2 TBS sugar.

8. Drop a tablespoonful of the mixture onto each dough circle and fold the dough up over the filling. Pinch the dough to seal it.

9. Fry in hot (360 degree) deep fat until golden brown. The temperature can be determined by using a candy thermometer.

10. Drain and sprinkle with powdered sugar. Serve hot.

Note: Instead of frying these may be baked in a preheated 400 degree oven for 20 minutes.

SOURDOUGH PEACH GOODIES

Peaches baked in a sourdough leavened dough comprise these great breakfast or desert treats.

> 1 cup Room Temperature Sourdough Starter
> 4 eggs beaten
> 2 TBS melted butter
> 2-2½ cups white flour
> ¼ tsp salt
> 6 peach halves
> (canned peach halves should be drained before use)

Yield: 6 individual delightful peach filled breakfast rolls.

1. Prepare the Room Temperature Sourdough Starter following the directions in Chapter 4. Be sure to replenish your original starter before proceeding with the recipe.

2. Assemble all ingredients and utensils. Let all ingredients come to room temperature.

3. Place the 1 cup of starter in a 2-quart or larger bowl. Add the 4 beaten eggs and 2 TBS of melted butter.

4. Stir in the ¼ tsp salt and 2 to 2½ cups of white flour ½ cup at a time until the dough is soft and sticky. Do not add more flour than to bring it to the sticky and soft point.

5. Pat the dough out to about ¼ inch thickness. Using a saucer as a pattern cut out circles of 4 to 5 inch diameter.

6. Place a peach half on each. If you are using fresh peaches fill each one with 1 tsp sugar.

7. Fold the dough up over the peach to cover it and pinch the dough to seal it. Place with the seam down on a greased cookie sheet.

8. Brush the outside of each with milk and bake in a preheated 375 degree oven for 45 minutes.

9. When done remove from oven and place on wire racks to cool. When cool frost with a sugar icing.

SOURDOUGH BLACKBERRY COBBLER

1½ cups Primary Batter "B"
    or Room Temperature Sourdough Starter
2½ cups flour
1 tsp salt
½ cup shortening
blackberry filling
Yield: 1 cobbler.

1. Prepare the Primary Batter "B" or Room Temperature Sourdough Starter following the directions in Chapter 4.

2. Assemble all ingredients and utensils. Let all ingredients come to room temperature.

3. Put the 2½ cups of flour into a large bowl. Stir 1 tsp salt into the flour.

4. Cut ¼ cup of shortening into the flour until it resembles coarse cornmeal.

5. Add the 1½ cups of Primary Batter "B" while stirring with a wooden spoon. Work all the flour and batter together until it is one big ball of dough.

6. Divide the dough into two parts, one of which is a little larger than the other. Roll the larger half into a rectangle about 12x16 inches and line a 9x13x2 baking pan with it. The pan does not need to be greased.

7. Pour in your favorite blackberry filling.

8. Roll the remaining dough into a 9x13 inch rectangle and cut slits in it as you would in a pie crust. Place this on top of the filling. Moisten the edges of the top crust and then fold the lining crust over these moistened edges.

9. Bake in a preheated 375 degree oven for 30 minutes or until brown.

Note: This recipe adapts to any filling which you would use in a cobbler. Cherry, apple and peach are other fillings which make good cobblers.

SOURDOUGH ENGLISH PLUM PUDDING

For a different desert serve this version of the traditional plum pudding.

1 cup Room Temperature Sourdough Starter
½ lb suet
½ tsp nutmeg
½ tsp allspice
½ tsp salt
½ tsp baking soda
1½ cups currants
½ cup mixed candied fruit
3 eggs well beaten
1 cup flour
1 cup brown sugar

Yield: 1 large loaf.

1. Prepare the Room Temperature Sourdough Starter following the directions in Chapter 4. Be sure to replenish your original starter before proceeding with the recipe.

2. Assemble all ingredients and utensils. Let all ingredients come to room temperature.

3. Chop the suet finely, or run it through a meat grinder. Add the 1 cup of flour to the suet along with the ½ tsp nutmeg, ½ tsp allspice, ½ tsp salt and ½ tsp baking soda. Stir.

4. Separate the currants and candied fruit and stir them into the flour mixture.

5. Beat the eggs until frothy and stir in 1 cup brown sugar, ½ tsp soda and the 1 cup of sourdough starter. Blend well and add to flour mixture and mix well — this is a soft mixture.

6. Pour the batter into a well greased mold. A 2 lb. coffee can is the right size. Be sure to use a regular mold for this purpose of cans which do not have a coating on the inside. Cover the can or mold with wax paper fastened with a rubber band or with foil.

7. Place the mold on a rack in a pan of boiling water. The water should come halfway up the sides of the mold. Cover the pan and steam for 3 hours by keeping the water gently boiling. Replenish the water when necessary to keep it at the halfway level (be sure to add boiling water).

8. When the three hours are up, remove the mold from the boiling water and place in a 350 degree oven for 10 minutes.

9. Let cool and wrap in foil for storage. Brandy or sherry may be added every couple of weeks if you are going to store pudding for a long period of time.

10. When ready to serve, grease the mold and place the pudding back into it. Tightly cover the mold and then steam the pudding for 1 hour. Serve hot.

SOURDOUGH BOREK

This recipe makes little twists of sweet dough which puff when fried.

> 1 cup Room Temperature Sourdough Starter
> 3 egg yolks
> ¼ cup superfine sugar
> 2 TBS brandy (optional)
> ¼ cup yogurt
> ½ tsp salt
> 2½ cups white flour

Yield: About 72 pastries

1. Prepare the Room Temperature Sourdough Starter following the directions in Chapter 4. Be sure to replenish your original starter before proceeding with the recipe.

2. Assemble all ingredients and utensils. Let all ingredients come to room temperature.

3. Beat the 3 egg yolks until frothy.

4. Add the ¼ cup of superfine sugar and 2 TBS of brandy. Stir gently.

5. Add the ¼ cup of yogurt, 1 cup starter, ½ tsp salt and 1½ cups of white flour. Stir until the dough is mixed very well.

6. Turn the dough out onto a well floured board and knead in approximately 1 cup of white flour. Knead until the dough blisters.

7. Roll out as thin as possible. Cut the dough into ribbons which are about 1 inch wide. Cut these ribbons into 3 inch lengths.

8. Make a 1 inch slit lengthwise in each one and pull one end through the hole.

9. Fry in hot (385 degrees - determined by use of a candy thermometer) deep fat until golden brown. Turn once during frying.

10. Drain well and sprinkle with confectioners sugar.

SOURDOUGH SPICY OATMEAL PUDDING

1 cup Room Temperature Sourdough Starter
¾ cup sugar
¾ tsp salt
1 tsp baking soda
1 tsp cinnamon
1 cup quick cooking oatmeal
¾ cup chopped dates
3 TBS butter
1½ tsp vanilla

Yield: 6 servings.

1. Prepare the Room Temperature Sourdough Starter following the directions in Chapter 4. Be sure to replenish your original starter before proceeding with the recipe.

2. Assemble all ingredients and utensils. Let all ingredients come to room temperature.

3. Put the 1 cup of sourdough starter in a 2-quart bowl. Stir in ¾ cup sugar, ¾ tsp salt, 1 tsp baking soda and 1 tsp cinnamon.

4. Stir in 1 cup quick cooking oatmeal, ¾ cup dates chopped, 3 TBS butter and 1½ tsp vanilla. Stir until well mixed.

5. Grease a 1-quart pudding mold or a 1 pound coffee can. Pour the batter into the mold.

6. Cover the mold with two layers of wax paper or foil and hold in place with a rubber band.

7. Place the mold on a rack or trivet in a pan of boiling water. The water should come half way up the can or mold. Cover the pan of boiling water and steam for l½ hours.

8. When the steaming time is up remove from can by cutting out the bottom and pushing the pudding out onto a serving dish. Serve with a lemon sauce made by the following recipe.

Lemon Sauce

¼ cup sugar
1 TBS cornstarch
1 cup water
2 TBS melted butter
1½ TBS lemon juice
1/8 tsp salt

1. Put the ¼ cup sugar, 1 TBS cornstarch and 1 cup of water into the top half of a double boiler. Heat until thickened stirring constantly.

2. Remove from heat and stir in 2 TBS melted butter, 1½ TBS lemon juice and 1/8 tsp salt. Serve over the oatmeal pudding.

Chapter 15
SOURDOUGH STARTER IN BREAD MACHINES

America's love affair with bread has entered a new era. Fresh hot bread can now be had with little or no work! There are many brands of bread machines on the market with more arriving every day. Goldrush sourdough starter can be used in all bread machines. Mouth watering sourdough bread is only a push button away.

The following recipes call for sourdough starter. This refers to the full strength starter that you are keeping in your refrigerator. Bread machines work differently than a "hand baking" operation.

There are three basic bread machine sizes: one lb., 1½ lb. and two lb. loaves. Choose the recipe size that most closely approximates the capacity of your machine. You will get the best results when you do not exceed the capacity of your machine.

(All ingredients at room temperature)

	1 lb.	**1½ lb.**	**2 lb.**
Sourdough starter	¾ cup	1⅛ cups	1⅓ cups
water	¼ cup	⅓ cups	½ cups
vegetable oil	1 TBS	1⅓ TBS	2 TBS
salt	½ tsp	¾ tsp	1 tsp
sugar	1 TBS	1⅓ TBS	1½ TBS
bread flour	2 cups	3 cups	3½ cups
yeast (active dry)	1½ tsp	2 tsp	2 tsp

1. Place ingredients into your machine following manufacturer's directions.

2. Set your machine to basic white or sweet cycle and medium crust setting and push the start button. For the best bread do not use the rapid bake cycle.

3. Allow the machine to knead for approximately five minutes. Lift the lid and observe the consistency of the dough. The dough should form a well rounded ball which is soft but not sticky to the touch. If necessary, adjust the dough while the machine is kneading by adding one tablespoon of flour or water at a time until the dough ball is formed.

4. Allow the machine to complete the bread. Let the loaf cool. Enjoy!

Index

Notes

Notes

Notes